Study Guide

for use with

From Slavery to Freedom
A History of African Americans

Eighth Edition

John Hope Franklin
Duke University

Alfred A. Moss, Jr.
University of Maryland

Prepared by
Alfred A. Moss, Jr.
University of Maryland

Christopher Meagher
University of Colorado - Denver

Boston   Burr Ridge, IL   Dubuque, IA   Madison, WI   New York   San Francisco   St. Louis
Bangkok   Bogotá   Caracas   Lisbon   London   Madrid
Mexico City   Milan   New Delhi   Seoul   Singapore   Sydney   Taipei   Toronto

McGraw-Hill Higher Education

A Division of The McGraw-Hill Companies

Study Guide for use with FROM SLAVERY TO FREEDOM:
A HISTORY OF AFRICAN AMERICANS, EIGHTH EDITION

This book is printed on acid-free paper.

2 3 4 5 6 7 8 9 BKM BKM 9 0 9 8 7 6 5 4 3 2 1 0

ISBN 0-07-229586-4

www.mhhe.com

TABLE OF CONTENTS

PREFACE..iv
CHAPTER 1 Land of Their Ancestors 1
CHAPTER 2 The African Way of Life 8
CHAPTER 3 The Slave Trade and the New World 15
CHAPTER 4 Colonial Slavery 24
CHAPTER 5 That All May Be Free 31
CHAPTER 6 Blacks in the New Republic 39
CHAPTER 7 Blacks and Manifest Destiny 47
CHAPTER 8 That Peculiar Institution 55
CHAPTER 9 Quasi-Free Blacks...63
CHAPTER 10 Slavery and Intersectional Strife........................71
CHAPTER 11 The Civil War 81
CHAPTER 12 The Effort to Attain Peace 91
CHAPTER 13 Losing the Peace 101
CHAPTER 14 Philanthropy and Self-Help 110
CHAPTER 15 The Color Line...120
CHAPTER 16 In Pursuit of Democracy...................................128
CHAPTER 17 Democracy Escapes..136
CHAPTER 18 The Harlem Renaissance 144
CHAPTER 19 The New Deal..152
CHAPTER 20 The American Dilemma 161
CHAPTER 21 Fighting for the Four Freedoms........................173
CHAPTER 22 African Americans in the Cold War Era...........183
CHAPTER 23 The Black Revolution..195
CHAPTER 24 Reaction and Progress.......................................211
CHAPTER 25 Half Century of Change.....................................221
ANSWER KEY 231

PREFACE

This study guide was prepared to assist students with their reading of *From Slavery to Freedom*, eighth edition. Each of the twenty-five chapters contains a brief chronology, a chapter summary, chapter review questions, identifications, and a self-test section.

These different sections of the study guide can be used in a variety of ways, depending on both your needs and the requirements of your class. We suggest that you initially read the chapter summaries of this study guide in order to familiarize your self with the most prominent themes and developments discussed in each chapter of the textbook. Next, read the chapter assigned by your instructor. After you have completed an initial reading, the study guide questions and identifications will help you to focus on some of the more significant facts and developments of African-American history. Once you've completed these steps, test your comprehension by answering the self-test questions.

You will soon discover that some of the chapters of this review guide are considerably longer than others. This is a function of two factors: first, certain periods of African-American history have had greater and more enduring significance to the lives of both black and white Americans than have others. The Civil War, Reconstruction, and the post–World War II Civil Rights Movement are three such examples. Second, from 1865 until the 1960s, the literacy rate of African Americans expanded exponentially. Concomitant with this was the expansion of written records and of popular and scholarly studies of race relations in the United States; both developments allowed for a far richer understanding of the complexities of African-American life, and this helps explain why more recent African-American history is amply detailed.

We hope that your studies of African-American history will enable you to apprehend both the tragedies and triumphs, as well as the privations and pride, that have shaped the character of Americans of African descent living in the United States today.

Christopher Meagher
Alfred Moss
September 1999

CHAPTER 1
LAND OF THEIR ANCESTORS

THEMES AND MAJOR POINTS

For information on the early history of Africa and its many different communities, each with its distinctive political, social, and religious practices, historians are dependent on the observations of travelers and on oral tradition.

The state of Ghana was for a time a prosperous center of agriculture and trade. Many of its people and some of its rulers were Muslims. In the eleventh century, Tenkamenen, perhaps the greatest of Ghana's early kings, was very wealthy and ruled over a vast empire.

Eventually, the kingdom of Mali surpassed the heights that Ghana had reached. The great king and warrior Sundiata Keita made Mali into a wealthy empire, predominantly agricultural but also a society with skilled and productive craftpersons and miners. Some of Mali's kings were Muslims who made pilgrimages to Mecca, among them Mansa-Musa.

In the fifteenth century, thanks to the conquests of the warrior-king Sonni Ali, the kingdom of Songhay dominated West Africa. Songhay's most brilliant ruler, however, was Askia Mohammed, who devoted his energies to strengthening his empire, making his people prosperous, and encouraging learning.

Some of the other notable African states included the Mossi confederation; the seven states of the Afno or Hausa people; the communities of the people of Kanem and Bornu; the lands of the Bantu, San, Khokhoi, and Pygmies; and several states located from the mouth of the Niger around to the Cape of Good Hope. Complex and significant African communities were also found in the southern portions of the continent and on its east coast. To a greater or lesser degree, all of

Africa's communities had some connection with supplying North and South America with black people.

KEY EVENTS

1062   Reign of Ghana's Tenkamenin began.

1076   Muslim Almoravids invaded Ghana.

1235   Mali (Melle) began as an organized Kingdom.

1312   Reign of Mansa-Musa began in Mali.

1469   Songhay ruler Sonni Ali captured Timbuktu.

1493   Askia Mohammed became ruler of Songhay.

CHAPTER OVERVIEW

From the seventh century A.D. until the sixteenth century several powerful African states evolved. Of central importance were the nations of Ghana, Mali, and Songhay. These powerful kingdoms, like many other African states, were influenced to some degree by Islamic traditions and institutions; likewise, each kingdom influenced both the Arab people and other African people to the north, east, and south.

REVIEW QUESTIONS

Chapter Content Review

1.   What was the first West African state of which there is any record? What other major states arose in this region?

2. What was the chief town/commercial center of Ghana during the Middle Ages?

3. What non-African group first entered West Africa around the tenth century? What religion did they introduce?

4. What products did Ghana exchange for the Muslim textiles, salt, brass, pearls, and other products?

5. Who was Tenkamenin? What type of authority did he have?

6. Explain the reasons for the decline of the kingdom of Ghana from the eleventh to the thirteenth centuries.

7. What was a mansa? Which dynasty ruled Mali during the thirteenth and fourteenth centuries? Who was Sundiata Keita?

8. What contributions did Mansa-Musa and his successors make to the nation of Mali?

9. Who was Sonni Ali? By what means was Sonni Ali able to subdue the entire Niger region?

10. Why was Sonni Ali's reign over the Kingdom of Songhay filled with fighting?

11. Who was Askia Mohammed? How did he improve his empire?

12. What was the cultural significance of Timbuktu and Jenne?

13. What enabled the empire of Wagadugu (the Mossi states) to survive from about the eleventh century until the nineteenth century?

Identification Questions

You should be able to describe the following key terms, concepts, individuals, and places and explain their significance:

1. Sisse dynasty
2. mansas
3. Suleiman
4. Askia Mohammed
5. Timbuktu
6. Mossi States
7. Benin
8. Yoruba
9. Empire of the Congo

Essay Questions

1. Explain why European people prior to the eighteenth century would view Africa as the "dark continent." Given the political cultures of the West African states of Ghana, Mali, and Songhay, is this view accurate?

2. Discuss the impact of Islam on the African states after the tenth century.

SELF-TEST

Multiple-Choice

1. The first West African state, according to existing records, was
    a. Ghana.
    b. Mali.
    c. Zanzibar.
    d. Songhay.

2. The commercial center and chief town of the Ghanaians during the Middle Ages was
    a. Kumbi Saleh.
    b. Timbuktu.
    c. Wagadu.
    d. Bambuhu.

3. The first non-black African cultural group to influence Ghana was
    a. Greek.
    b. Arab.
    c. Hindu.
    d. Roman.

4. What legendary figure was credited with consolidating and strengthening the Kingdom of Mali in the thirteenth century?
    a. Sundiata Keita
    b. Mansa-Musa
    c. Tenkamenin

5. Who was Songhay's most brilliant ruler?
    a. Sonni Ali
    b. Idris Alooma
    c. Askia Mohammed

Fill-in-the Blank

1. Ethiopians have a recorded history almost _____ years old.

2. To the east and west of Lake Chad resided the people of _____.

3. Traders from _____ visited the markets of Timbuktu and Gao regularly.

4. The people of Mali were predominantly agricultural, but a substantial number were engaged in _____.

5. Arab writers say that Tenkamenin lived in a _____ made beautiful by sculpture, pictures, and windows decorated by royal artists.

True/False

1. The first major West African state in recorded history was Songhay.

2. The legendary Malian leader credited with consolidating and strengthening the Kingdom of Mali was Sundiata Keita.

3. One of the chief Ghanan exports during the Sisse dynasty was gold.

4. Slavery did not exist in western Africa prior to the arrival of Europeans.

5. The West African people of Mali, Songhay, and Ghana were heavily influenced by Christianity.

Relevance Today

1.   For information on the early history of Africa, historians depend heavily on oral traditions. How has oral history been used to recover the history of groups in the United States, such as the American Indians and the African American slave community.

2.   African communities were deeply affected by trade with the Arabic communities. Can you think of ways in which the various ethnic and racial communities in this country have been affected by U.S. trade with other nations?

3.   Powerful kings and military rulers were central figures in African states. Have such leaders played an important role in the history of blacks in the United States? If so, how? If not, why not?

CHAPTER 2
THE AFRICAN WAY OF LIFE

THEMES AND MAJOR POINTS

- African political organizations ranged in size and complexity, from the simple family state to the vast empires of Mali and Songhay.

- Even when they were part of larger kingdoms, local kings enjoyed considerable sovereignty over their own geographic area.

- The diverse economic behaviors, common to the African way of life, fueled extensive commercial networks both among African communities and with non-African people.

- Family economic behaviors determined the position an African man or woman enjoyed within the social strata common on the continent.

- The clan was the primary social unit of African communities, and this kinship unit had importance in African economic, political, and religious customs.

- While musical and artistic forms, as well as oral traditions, demonstrated high levels of cultural achievement, the great variety of spoken languages inhibited the development of literary forms.

- Despite the heterogeneity of cultures, African people still had sufficient homogeneity of experiences to enable them to cooperate in the New World. Consequently, they fashioned new customs and traditions which reflected their African roots.

KEY EVENTS

1500–1800   African cultural forms transplanted to the New World.
Tarikh-es Soudan, a history of Sudan, was written by
Es-Sadi.
Tarikh-El-Fettach, was written by Kati, a Sudanese.

CHAPTER OVERVIEW

On the eve of the sixteenth century, Africa teemed with a rich diversity of cultures. Across the continent could be found stable political structures, diversified economies, and cohesive social institutions. Whether the states were great empires or modest political entities, they were generally well organized and able to maintain law, order, and social harmony. This political stability both within and among the African states was conducive to healthy economic development. The Africans, whether farmers or artisans, displayed remarkable versatility and varieties of talents and tastes.

Most impressive in considering the social institutions of Africa was the cohesive influence of the family. The immediate family, the clan, and the tribe undergirded every aspect of life. The influence and hold the patriarch had over the members of the family was largely responsible for the stability which was characteristic of the area. The deep loyalty and attachment of the individual to the family approached reverence and, indeed, was the basis for most religious practices. Thus, the world "discovered" by the fifteenth-century Europeans was already highly civilized.

REVIEW QUESTIONS

Chapter Content Review

1. From which area of Africa did the vast majority of slaves originate?

2. What were the essential characteristics of the African village states?

3. What economic activities were common in Africa? What impact did commerce have on Africa?

4. Was Africa polygamist, monogamist, or a combination? What was usually the determining factor?

5. What was the basis for most social stratification in Africa?

6. Which Africans were or became slaves in Africa? Did the children of slaves have any rights?

7. Before the arrival of Islam, what was the most common form of African religion? What religious rituals did the Africans practice?

8. Where did Islam have its greatest success on the African continent?

9. What impeded the spread of Islam and Christianity to central and Western Africa?

10. What inhibited the development of literary forms in Africa?

11. By what means were the multitude of African stories, histories, and myths transmitted to later generations, both before and after the Muslim incursion?

12.   What significance did the family have in the African social structure?

Identification Questions

You should be able to describe the following key terms, concepts, individuals, and places and explain their significance:

1.   clan
2.   ancestor worship
3.   Suto/Ruanda/Banda
4.   Es-Sadi and Kati
5.   drum/guitar/zither

Essay Questions

1.   Discuss the political, economic, and social structures of African life that the observant European trader or missionary would have encountered in the sixteenth century.

2.   In what ways were the political, economic, and social structures of thirteenth- to sixteenth-century Africa similar to those of late medieval and early modern Europe?

SELF-TEST

Multiple-Choice

1.   In early African society, the eldest male was
        a.   usually the head of the family.
        b.   always the head of the family.
        c.   never the head of the family.
        d.   only rarely the head of the family.

2. The practice of polygamy in early Africa was
   a. forbidden.
   b. denied to the converts of Islam.
   c. permitted in virtually every region.
   d. encouraged by Christian missionaries.

3. The monarchs of West African political units were
   a. rarely absolute rulers.
   b. elected on the basis of universal manhood suffrage.
   c. seldom, if ever, limited in their power.
   d. always the eldest son of the royal family.

4. In which region of Africa did Islam spread with notable success in the eighth century?
   a. West Africa
   b. South Africa
   c. East Africa
   d. North Africa

5. The priests in the African religions were the _____ of the family.
   a. matriarchs
   b. patriarchs
   c. goldsmiths
   d. physicians

6. Practices common to African religions included
   a. animism.
   b. ancestor veneration.
   c. belief in a creator spirit.
   d. all of the above.

Fill-in-the-Blank

1.   The _____ was the most basic unit of social organization in early Africa.

2.   The most common form of government in the early African societies was _____.

3.   The practice of polygamy in Africa was opposed by the influence of _____ in Africa.

4.   Many of the African oral traditions were written in _____ after the fourteenth century.

True/False

1.   Africans were neither primarily nomadic nor simply agricultural.

2.   The use of iron developed very early in African economies.

3.   The African clan or enlarged family was composed of all families that claimed a common ancestor.

4.   Africa between 700 and 1400 was a land almost totally isolated from the non-African world.

5.   Slavery was not an important feature in either African economic or social life.

Relevance Today

1.   Political checks and balances have become standard features of all North American governing systems since the Constitution. What features of African political systems exemplify this practice?

2. Social stratification has been a constant feature of African communities. Are African-American communities stratified today? If so, what determines the relative position of each group, and how difficult is it to achieve upward mobility?

3. Franklin and Moss assert that African religious practices were very resilient, despite pressures to convert to Islam or Christianity. What pressures do African-American communities resist steadfastly today? When is this good? When is this bad?

CHAPTER 3
THE SLAVE TRADE AND THE NEW WORLD

THEMES AND MAJOR POINTS

Slavery was widespread during the earliest known history of Africa as well as of other continents. The Muslim invasion of Africa hastened the development of slavery because it stimulated the exportation of Africans as slaves to other parts of the world.

In Europe the Renaissance, which sanctioned the rights of individuals to pursue their own benefit even if this involved the exploitation of others, and the Commercial Revolution, which led to fierce economic competition between European countries, generated forces that created the modern institution of slavery and the slave trade.

Europeans used Christianity as one of the rationales for their activities as slaveholders and slave traders. The Portuguese and Spaniards were the earliest to justify their actions as a form of Christian missionary work. European slave traders argued that, through forced conversion and transplantation to European settlements, African slaves were brought into the Christian community and led to a knowledge of the true God.

The conquered Indian nations were first used by European colonists as slaves. Indian slavery was a failure, however, because of the high death rate of enslaved Indians, the relatively small size of the Indian population, and the resistance of unconquered Indian nations.

To compensate for the shortage of workers, Europeans brought poor whites as indentured servants from Europe, voluntarily and involuntarily, to do heavy labor. White indentured servants expressed their dissatisfaction through court challenges and by running away. The dissatisfaction of white indentured servants and the refusal of most poor whites to come to the colonies as indentured servants caused this labor system to fail.

African captives came to be seen by Europeans as ideal slaves: their color made it easy to catch them if they ran away; it was legal to purchase and hold them as workers permanently; and because they were not Christians, whites were free to discipline them rigidly, as well as morally and spiritually degrade them, with little or no interference from the state or church.

During the seventeenth and eighteenth centuries, the African slave trade emerged as one of the most important and lucrative forms of international business. The nations that led the way in developing and expanding this trade were the Dutch, the French, and the English. The voyage of slave ships to the Americas, popularly referred to as the "middle passage," was a veritable nightmare.

The slave trade was directly responsible for the development of the plantation system and the slave societies in the Caribbean Islands and mainland South and North America.

KEY EVENTS

1300s Commercial Revolution began.

1390   African slaves were brought to Europe.

1493   Pope Alexander VI created demarcation line dividing the nonEuropean world between Spain and Portugal.

1517   Bartolemeo de Las Casas advocated encouragement of African immigration to the New World.

1520s Estevanico explored New Mexico and Arizona for the Spanish.

1619   First African indentures were sold in the Virginia colony.

1640s   West Indian sugar plantations arose.

1672   Royal African Company was chartered by the king of England.

CHAPTER OVERVIEW

Although the institution of slavery had existed for millennia and in a diversity of regions, it attained its brutal apex after the dawn of the European Commercial Revolution. Beginning the fifteenth and sixteenth centuries, Portuguese and Spanish sea-farers established prosperous trading posts along the coast of West Africa. In addition to the spices, gold, ivory, and agricultural products available, the Iberians perceived the potential of African slaves as surrogates for the decimated Indian laborers in the New World. By the seventeenth century, the Spanish had created an American empire, heavily dependent on this slave labor.

Spanish dominance of the West Indies ended with the encroachments of Denmark, Britain, France, and the Netherlands upon the Spanish slave trade monopoly. These other nations eventually competed vigorously for the profits derived from both the slave trade and the fruits of West Indian slave labor: tobacco, indigo, and cotton. After 1640, the substantial profits derived from the sugar plantations engendered a virtual flooding of the West Indies with African slaves. Throughout this region the institution of slavery varied depending on time, ratio of slaves to whites, cost of slaves and market price for a given crop, and other factors, yet in all regions of the Americas slavery represented abject and inhuman cruelty.

REVIEW QUESTIONS

Chapter Content Review

1. In what capacity did the Muslim political and economic elites use African slaves?

2. In what ways did the Renaissance and the Commercial Revolution in Europe create the modern system of slavery and the slave trade?

3. Which European countries during the fifteenth century created the foundation for the African slave trade of later years? How did they justify their actions?

4. Where did Africans play significant roles in the process of exploring and discovering America?

5. Why was Indian slavery in the New World unprofitable?

6. Why did white indentured servitude prove unsatisfactory?

7. What advantages were there in resorting to African labor in the American colonies?

8. By the eighteenth century, which nation had clearly emerged as the dominant slave trader?

9. In what ways did the introduction of European weaponry influence the future of Western Africa?

10. In what region of the New World was the first complement of slaves sent? Why were they sent there?

11. Which European countries broke the Spanish monopoly of the slave trade in the West Indies in both the sixteenth and seventeenth centuries?

12. What were the consequences of the Dutch proposal that the West Indies planters begin growing sugar cane?

13. For what reason did the planters of the West Indies overpopulate their plantations with slaves?

14. What effect did absentee landlordism have on typical slave living conditions in the West Indies?

15. Describe the diet and the working conditions typical for West Indian slaves.

16. What factors led to the increase in exportation of slaves from the West Indies to the American mainland?

17. In what economic pursuits were Brazilian slaves employed?

Identification Questions

You should be able to describe the following key terms, concepts, individuals, and places and explain their significance:

1. Estevanico
2. Negroes de Gano
3. Bartolomeo de Las Casas
4. caboceer
5. "middle passage"
6. absentee landlordism
7. seasoning process
8. Maroons
9. Macandal

10. asiento
11. Viceroyalty of New Granada
12. mestizos
13. Jean Baptiste Point du Sable

Essay Questions

1. In what ways did eighteenth- and nineteenth-century Latin American slavery differ from slavery on the British mainland?

2. What effects did the slave trade have on West Africa and the future of African civilizations?

SELF-TEST

Multiple-Choice

1. Important to the slave trade was
    a. the active cooperation of certain African chiefs.
    b. the desire of large numbers of Africans to migrate to the West Indies.
    c. the friendly relationship between Christian missionaries and Muslims.
    d. the convenient overland route between West and North Africa.

2. According to Professor Philip D. Curtin, the total number of slaves imported to the New World between 1451 and 1870 was (approximately)
    a. 1,340,000.
    b. 6,050,000.
    c. 9,500,000.
    d. 1,900,000.

3. Plantation slaves in the West Indies were
   a. most often supervised directly by their owners.
   b. engaged primarily in the cultivation of cotton.
   c. generally left in the hands of overseers whose chief concern was to produce wealth for their employers.
   d. seldom discontented with their lot.

4. The following nations dominated the slave trade:
   a. Spain and Portugal
   b. Italy, Belgium, and Ireland
   c. Dutch traders, France, and England

5. The *asiento* gave Spanish traders permission
   a. to bring slaves into Spanish colonies.
   b. to lead armies of conquest to North and South America.
   c. to transport missionaries to the Spanish colonies.

Fill-in-the-Blank

1. Runaway slaves in such places as Haiti and Jamaica were called
   _____.

2. _____ referred to the process of "breaking-in" newcomers to the islands' slave population.

3. _____ were Europeans who, in exchange for their passage to the New World, voluntarily sold their labor for a specified period of time.

4. _____ was the black explorer who is credited with opening New Mexico and Arizona for the Spaniards.

5. Perhaps the largest concentration of blacks in continental Spanish America was to be found in _____.

True/False

1. Of all European nations, Portugal realized the greatest profits from the slave trade.

2. Africans were first used in the West Indies to cultivate sugar cane.

3. Africans offered stiff resistance to their capture, sale, and transportation to the New World.

4. The major cause of disease and epidemic on slave ships traveling from Africa to the Americas was the shortage of medicine.

5. The Africans the traders sought for slaves were the healthiest, the largest, the youngest, the ablest, and the most culturally advanced.

Relevance Today

1. The enslavement of Africans was influenced by Europeans' belief in the rights of individuals to pursue their advantage, even if this involved the exploitation of others and fierce economic competition between European countries. Are there people in the United States today who believe in the right of individuals to pursue their benefit even if this involves the exploitation of others? If so, how does this influence how the strong treat the weak in our country? What role does the fierce economic competition between the United States and other countries at the present time influence how the strong treat the weak in the United States?

2. African captives came to be seen by Europeans as ideal slaves because of the ways in which they were different from Europeans. In the United States today, how have differences between various kinds of Americans (African Americans, Asian Americans, European Americans, Latino Americans, and Native Americans, among others) come to be appreciated as positive qualities that contribute to the

strength of the United States? Are there currently some differences among various American ethnic and racial groups that some citizens of the United States see as negative?

3. European colonists accepted slavery as the answer to their need for a large supply of cheap labor. How is the need for a cheap labor pool in the United States met today?

CHAPTER 4
COLONIAL SLAVERY

THEMES AND MAJOR POINTS

- In the Chesapeake region of the New World, African slavery arose in response to the labor needs of the emerging tobacco economy.

- Colonial legislation in the Chesapeake region denigrated the political status of African people, and their slave status was guaranteed by enforced slave codes.

- Because of the brutality committed against Africans held in bondage, violent rebellions arose periodically; these were virtually always put down with even greater acts of violence and repression.

- Although slavery spread to both the Middle and New England colonies, it failed to secure a foothold in those regions.

- Slavery was commercially significant to the New England colonies, primarily because of the lucrative slave trading conducted by New England shipowners.

- Blacks in New England, slave and free, did not face the same harsh codes and rigid social restrictions that were mandated by Southern legislatures.

- Institutionalized slavery became a hallmark of Southern culture during the colonial period, and the slave-master relationship would become a model for all relations in the region.

KEY EVENTS

1619   First Africans were sold to British in Virginia.

1638   First Africans were brought into New England.

1661   Virginia enacted law to sanction slavery.

1712, 1741   Slave insurrections occurred in New York.

1739   Stono Rebellion erupted in South Carolina.

1750   Georgia repealed its prohibition against slavery.

CHAPTER OVERVIEW

In 1619, the first Africans transported to the mainland British
American colonies were received as indentured servants. Over the next
fifty years the status of their descendants and other Africans in the
Chesapeake colonies would diminish to the level of chattel slaves. Like
slavery in the West Indies, British colonial slavery proved to be a
convenient substitute for white and Indian labor along the southern
Atlantic coast. In Virginia and Maryland, successful subjugation of the
Africans, coupled with increasing agricultural wealth, stimulated the
expansion of slavery into the Carolinas and Georgia, especially after 1700.

Slavery was introduced to the Middle Colonies and New England
in the first half of the seventeenth century, yet, unlike the South, where
large slave populations engendered extensive fears of rebellion, slaves and
free blacks constituted only a small fraction of the population.

REVIEW QUESTIONS

Chapter Content Review

1.   What was the legal status of most Africans who landed in the Virginia colony prior to 1650?

2.   What accounts for the decline of the Africans' status in the Chesapeake region in the mid-seventeenth century and thereafter? What were some of the aspects of Virginia's slave code and why was it so harsh?

3.   Was the institution of slavery as it evolved in Maryland significantly different from that of Virginia? Explain.

4.   Were the Carolinas originally planned as a slave colony? Explain.

5.   Why did South Carolina have the most stringent slave code found in the British colonies?

6.   What impact did the Quakers have on the institution of slavery in North Carolina?

7.   How pervasive was slavery in the British North American colonies from 1680 to 1750? In which of the Middle Atlantic colonies did the largest number of slaves reside?

8.   Why was slavery unsuccessful in the Middle Colonies?

9.   Why were the New England slave codes that developed less stringent than the codes of other colonies?

Identification Questions

You should be able to describe the following key terms, concepts, individuals, and places and explain their significance:

1. Society for the Propagation of the Gospel in Foreign Parts
2. Stono Rebellion
3. slave codes
4. Society of Friends (Quakers)
5. Fundamental Constitution (of the Carolinas)
6. Royal African Company

Essay Questions

1. Compare and contrast the forms of slavery that emerged in the Caribbean Islands and the British American colonies north of Florida.

2. The settlers of the New World were predominately Christian people who felt duty bound to obey the laws of God. How could they have been both God-fearing Christians and participants in a slaving society?

SELF-TEST

Multiple-Choice

1. The twenty blacks who were brought to Jamestown in 1619
    a. were immediately deported.
    b. were slaves under existing Virginia law.
    c. were "seasoned" and then sent to the West Indies.
    d. occupied a position similar to that of the white indentures.

2. Three of the following answers concerning colonial slave codes are false. Which one is true?
    a. They provided the method by which masters could easily manumit slaves.
    b. They safeguarded the civil and political rights of slaves.
    c. They were regulatory and designed to suppress rebellion and control conduct.
    d. They generally permitted slaves freedom of movement and freedom of assembly.

3. During the Colonial Period, slavery was a legal institution
    a. only in the South.
    b. in all thirteen colonies.
    c. only in the Middle Colonies.
    d. in the southern and Middle Colonies, but not in New England.

4. What was the name of the company, chartered in 1672, that vastly increased the number of slaves in Virginia around the start of the eighteenth century?
    a. London Company
    b. Royal African Company
    c. British Slaving United
    d. Puritan Slave Company

5. The institution of slavery failed to root itself in the Middle Colonies because
    a. few slaves ever landed in New York, the chief port town.
    b. unlike Southern gentlemen, people in the Middle Colonies lacked the wealth needed to purchase slave labor.
    c. the subsistent agricultural economy of the Middle Colonies did not encourage the large-scale employment of slave labor.
    d. all of the above.

Fill-in-the-Blank

1.   The landing of blacks in the _____ colony marked the beginning of the forced importation of black people into the North American mainland.

2.   The _____ were a religious group largely responsible for the comparatively slow growth of slavery in Pennsylvania.

3.   _____ This region's primary interest in slavery came through the slave trade.

4.   _____ Two dramatic slave rebellions took place in this Middle Colony in the seventeenth century.

5.   The _____, penned by John Locke, claimed that freemen had total power over their slaves, regardless of a slave's religion.

6.   One striking contradiction to the harsh existence of slaves in _____ was the missionary organization called the Society for the Propagation of the Gospel in Foreign Parts.

True/False

1.   At the time it was founded, slavery was banned in the Carolinas.

2.   Statutory recognition of slavery in Virginia did not come until 1661.

3.   The relations between colonial Virginia and colonial Maryland in the eighteenth century were strained because Virginia' slaves could escape easily to Maryland, where slavery was illegal.

4.   The Middle Colony with the largest number of Africans was New York.

Relevance Today

1.   The early influx of slaves into Virginian society, followed by the influx of slaves into other parts of the colonial South, profoundly affected the psychological security of white colonists and typically led to political repression. What parallels exist between the rapid demographic change in the colonial South and the massive demographic changes that occurred in the twentieth century in the United States? When might majority groups in entrenched power positions welcome minority groups?

2.   Franklin and Moss repeatedly refer to the economic forces that engendered and bolstered colonial slavery. What evidence is there, from your own experience or from American culture in general, that economics stimulate immoral behaviors?

3.   Chapter 4 highlights differences that existed among both the different regions and the different colonies with respect to slavery. Does the region one is from today have as much impact on the shaping of cultural practices as it did in colonial times?

CHAPTER 5
THAT ALL MAY BE FREE

THEMES AND MAJOR POINTS

As whites saw in England's colonial policy a threat to the economic and political freedom that they had enjoyed for generations, they also seemed to recognize a marked inconsistency in their position as oppressed colonists *and* slaveholders. The death of Crispus Attucks, a runaway slave, in the Boston Massacre, highlighted this inconsistency. He was a black who died for the cause of the colonists, yet who was not as free as whites.

Though the colonial leaders decided not to denounce slavery in the Declaration of Independence, black sailors served in the American navy and black soldiers served the cause of independence in every phase of the war and under every possible circumstance. African-American patriots, both free and slave, supported the Revolution, believing an American victory would not only secure political freedom for the colonies but also free blacks from slavery.

The impact of the American Revolution on race relations was seen in the manumission of blacks who had fought for independence of the colonies, the increase in the number of white manumission and antislavery societies, and the success of the movement to abolish slavery in the Northern states after the war.

Despite the efforts of antislavery leaders to eliminate slavery, they were unable to do so. Resistance to abolitionist schemes hardened in the Southern states, where so much capital was invested in slaves and the institution of slavery was acquiring a new economic importance. The federal constitution adopted by the thirteen states included the machinery and safeguards that ensured the continual enslavement of blacks.

KEY EVENTS

1763   French-Indian War ended

1764   Sugar Act imposed

1770   Boston Massacre occurred; Crispus Attucks was slain.

1775   Quakers organized first antislavery society.
Lord Dunsmore offered emancipation to those slaves who would fight the colonials.

1776   Declaration of Independence was signed.
Policy of excluding blacks from the Continental Army was repealed.

1787   Northwest Ordinance banned slavery in territory north of the Ohio River.
Constitutional Convention held.

CHAPTER OVERVIEW

By the end of the French-Indian War, slavery had become both a commonly accepted and an integral part of the colonial American economy.

Although heavily concentrated in the Southern colonies, slavery benefited Northern commercial interests. The French-Indian War, however, exposed the growing conflict between colonial economic and British imperial objectives. This conflict culminated in the British imposition of stringent economic controls on the colonials. Moreover, this assertion of arbitrary power engendered the American Revolution. The Revolution was a political, ideological, and armed struggle between the British and the British-American colonials, replete with passion over the notions of liberty, property, equality, and slavery.

The American Revolutionary Period of 1763–1776 saw the emergence of a broad-based antislavery movement, yet the antislavery movement at this time was fueled more by anti-British sentiment than by passionate commitment to the ideals of human liberty and equality. Despite the efforts of fervent Quakers and a multitude of antislavery societies during and after the years of the War for Independence, the forces of political compromise and conservatism would prevail at the nation's historic Constitutional Convention of 1787. Among the values of life, liberty, and property, property emerged preeminent; and the liberty of white men to possess black men as property was established as a first principle of the Republic.

REVIEW QUESTIONS

Chapter Content Review

1. How did the end of the French-Indian War usher in a new approach to the problem of slavery in the British-American colonies?

2. How did the British contribute to the growth of the antislavery movement?

3. What impact did American revolutionary ferment have on blacks in the mid-Atlantic and New England colonies?

4. Whom did Jefferson blame for the continuation of the slave trade in America (in the "Summary View of the Rights of British America")?

5. Why were the colonists increasingly willing to prohibit the importation of slaves from 1774 to 1776?

6. Explain why the colonials were or were not willing to prohibit the importation of slaves after 1776.

7.	Were blacks a part of the early revolutionary military efforts in Massachusetts?

8.	What factors compelled George Washington to reconsider his decision to prohibit the recruitment of blacks for the Continental Army?

9.	During the Revolutionary War, what impact did British occupation of slaveholding areas have on the institution of slavery?

10.	What effect did the Revolutionary War have on slavery?

11.	What benefits did the war bring some slaves?

12.	For what reasons did states refuse to permit enlistments by blacks?

13.	How did the all-black units of the Continental Army fare in battle?

14.	Why did South Carolina, but not Virginia, object so vigorously to the proposed abolition of the slave trade?

15.	Did the Constitution sanction the slave trade?

Identification Questions

You should be able to describe the following key terms, concepts, individuals, and places and explain their significance:

1.	Crispus Attucks
2.	Summary View of the Rights of British America
3.	Lord John Murray Dunmore
4.	Northwest Ordinance
5.	Three-Fifths Compromise

Essay Questions

1.   What social implications did the revolutionary ideas contain and how did these ideas influence state legislatures in the postwar years?

2.   What impact was the Revolutionary War likely to have on blacks who served in the patriots' cause? In what way would the black soldier view the war differently than the white soldier?

SELF-TEST

Multiple-Choice

1.   One passage of the original draft of the Declaration of Independence that Jefferson was persuaded to omit
        a.   declared all slaves free.
        b.   upheld the king's right to rule the colonies.
        c.   condemned slavery.
        d.   asserted that all men were created equal.

2.   All of the following were black soldiers who distinguished themselves in battle except:
        a.   Edward Rutledge.
        b.   Prince Hall.
        c.   Peter Salem.
        d.   Salem Poor.

3.   The Three-Fifths Compromise of the Constitution
        a.   reconciled the interests of creditors and debtors.
        b.   protected the African slave trade for a time.
        c.   stipulated that fugitive slaves be returned to masters.
        d.   provided for the counting of slaves for the purposes of representation in Congress and taxation.

4.   *The Patriot, Liberty, Tempest, Dragon,* and *Diligence* were
      a.   titles of songs sung by American patriots.
      b.   nicknames of blacks who fought for American
            independence.
      c.   American ships on which black sailors served.
      d.   blacks killed with Crispus Attucks in the Boston Massacre.

5.   Which state did not make provision for the gradual abolition of
      slavery after the war?
      a.   Pennsylvania
      b.   New Jersey
      c.   Connecticut
      d.   Delaware

Fill-in-the-Blank

1.   One of the two states opposed to the enlistment of black soldiers
      throughout the Revolutionary War was _____.

2.   The Royal Governor of Virginia who offered freedom to slaves in
      return for service to the British army was _____.

3.   The British policy of benign or salutary neglect came to an end
      with the conclusion of the _____ War in 1763.

4.   The New Jersey Quaker who spoke out against slavery was

      _____.

5.   At the Constitutional Convention _____ of
      Massachusetts attacked slavery in a fiery speech and condemned
      any proposal that would recognize it in the Constitution.

True/False

1. Since the bulk of the black population was in the South, the majority of black soldiers in the patriot armies came from this section.

2. The vast majority of black soldiers served in primarily white units during the Revolutionary War.

3. There are many instances of blacks serving in the Revolutionary navy during the War for Independence.

4. Manumission and antislavery societies became more numerous after the Revolutionary War.

5. At the Constitutional Convention, Charles Pinckney of South Carolina said his state would accept a constitution that prohibited the slave trade.

Relevance Today

1. On the eve of the Revolutionary War some Americans saw contradiction and inconsistency in their position as oppressed colonists and slaveholders. Can you think of ways in which there are contradictions between the beliefs and practices of Americans today?

2. Prior to and during the War for Independence, blacks did not have the same rights as whites; indeed, most were slaves, yet many blacks were ardent participants on the American side during the Revolutionary War. Why do you think many members of minority groups who are discriminated against today feel great allegiance to the United States and the American way of life? Why do other blacks not feel the same allegiance?

3.	One of the ways in which some Americans expressed their belief in the principles and values of the Revolutionary War was by fighting against slavery and purchasing the freedom of slaves. How do citizens of the United States living today put into practice their belief in their country's highest principles and values?

CHAPTER 6
BLACKS IN THE NEW REPUBLIC

THEMES AND MAJOR POINTS

- The African-American population was among the most thriving of any ethnic group in the United States during this period.

- Three distinct subcultures could be found in the postrevolutionary period: in the North, in the Chesapeake area, and in the deep South.

- The cotton gin breathed new life into cotton agriculture and, consequently, increased demand for slave labor.

- During the French Revolution, slaves in the West Indies effected their own emancipation by revolting against French authority.

- West Indian revolutions frightened American slave states to the north and discouraged the importation of slaves.

- Beginning with the revolutionary period, blacks not only sought ways of participating in the struggle for independence from England but also struggled to secure for themselves a measure of independence from white-dominated societies.

- The individual strivings of Jupiter Hammon, Phillis Wheatley, Benjamin Banneker, and Paul Cuffe represent both the efforts of blacks to secure a measure of independence for themselves in the postrevolutionary period and the movement of all Americans toward intellectual and economic self-sufficiency that was so characteristic of the period.

- Religious organizations, such as the Society of Friends, led the effort to promote educational opportunities for blacks in this period.

- African Americans in the postrevolutionary period rejected white domination of religious institutions and established their own institutions.

KEY EVENTS

1787	Free African Society organized.
1789	French Revolution commenced.
1791	Benjamin Banneker published his first almanac.
1791–1801	Rebellion of Santo Domingan slaves occurred.
1793	Cotton gin invented. Congress enacted Fugitive Slave Law.
1800	Toussaint L'Ouverture captured.
1803	Louisiana Purchase occurred.
1807	Congress enacted ban on the importation of slaves.

CHAPTER OVERVIEW

By the last decade of the nineteenth century, some 4 million people inhabited the United States. Of these people, 750,000 were of African descent and, of these, approximately 700,000 were owned by other human beings. Although slavery was gradually undergoing a process of obsolescence in the North at the turn of the century, the incessant lure of western land and effects of the Industrial Revolution would consign the great multitude of these "children of Africa" and their progeny to sixty more years of chattel slavery.

With the introduction of the cotton gin, new life was breathed into American slavery. The gin permitted an enormous expansion of cotton agriculture; coupled with the seemingly insatiable demand of British textile manufacturers, the need for field hands increased exponentially. Lured by high cotton prices, thousands rushed to secure land in the rich soils of the American Southwest. With an increasing demand for cotton laborers, the domestic slave trade burgeoned, and American participation in the international slave trade continued: legally before 1808 and illicitly thereafter. Slavery and the slave trade had become, by the early nineteenth century, an important cog in the wheel of American economic progress.

Simultaneous with the entrenchment of slavery evolved the commitment of free blacks to create their own social, religious, and educational institutions for the purposes of achieving a greater degree of independence, pride, and fulfillment. Black scientists, poets, writers, teachers, preachers, and abolitionists all struggled to both advance the cause of independence for black Americans and advance the intellectual, moral, and spiritual life of America.

REVIEW QUESTIONS

Chapter Content Review

1. Which state had the greatest number of slaves in 1790?

2. What twin evils plagued the post–Revolutionary War tobacco plantations?

3. What revolutionary advances in technology contributed to the sustenance of African slavery in America at the end of the eighteenth century?

4.   What made the transition from rice, indigo, or tobacco farming to cotton farming so easy?

5.   What role did New England merchants play in this movement toward cotton agriculture?

6.   How did the Southern states respond to the news of slave revolution in the West Indies beginning in 1791?

7.   What relevance did the government's purchase of Louisiana have on slavery in the United States?

8.   In 1807 the United States outlawed the slave trade. What impact did this legislation have?

9.   What groups in America established the first schools for blacks?

10.   What inhibited the development of schools for blacks in Virginia and the Carolinas around 1800?

11.   What factors contributed to the development of racially separate churches in America?

12.   What checked the growth of "Negro Methodism" in the South in the early nineteenth century?

13.   What opportunities did segregated worship provide for American blacks?

Identification Questions

You should be able to describe the following key terms, concepts, individuals, and places and explain their significance:

1. Eli Whitney
2. Toussaint L'Ouverture
3. General Le Clerc
4. Fugitive Slave Act of 1793
5. Stephen R. Bradley
6. Jupiter Hammon
7. Phillis Wheatley
8. Gustavus Vassa
9. Benjamin Banneker
10. James Derham
11. Paul Cuffe
12. Andrew Bryan
13. Richard Allen

Essay Questions

1. In what ways did segregation serve the interests of American blacks at the turn of the century? Focus on both developments in the West Indies and religious developments in the United States around the turn of the century.

2. The resiliency and adaptability of African Americans if amply demonstrated by black cultural achievements at the turn of the century. Explain.

SELF-TEST

Multiple-Choice

1. The black population of the new United States in 1790
    a. was concentrated in cities and towns.
    b. was essentially rural.
    c. included no free black men and women.
    d. numbered more than 1 million.

2. According to the census of 1790, the vast majority of blacks lived in the South Atlantic states. Where were blacks most numerous?
    a. Georgia
    b. South Carolina
    c. Virginia
    d. Maryland

3. An accomplished black man who was editor of almanacs and who served on the commission appointed to define the boundaries and lay out the streets of the District of Columbia was
    a. Prince Hall.
    b. Benjamin Banneker.
    c. Paul Cuffe.
    d. Richard Allen.

4. What twin evils plagued the tobacco plantations of the South after the Revolutionary War?
    a. high cost of labor and expensive land
    b. soil exhaustion and oversupply
    c. high labor costs and soil exhaustion
    d. undersupply and cheap labor costs

5.   This person's literary achievements exemplified not an attack on slavery but, rather, the search for independence through escape.
   a.   Phillis Wheatley
   b.   Jupiter Hammon
   c.   Paul Cuffe
   d.   Gustavus Vassa

6.   This mariner refused to pay taxes to the state of Massachusetts because it denied him suffrage. Thereafter, Massachusetts changed its laws to permit full citizenship to all taxpayers.
   a.   James Derham
   b.   Jupiter Hammon
   c.   Paul Cuffe
   d.   Gustavus Vassa

Fill-in-the-Blank

1.   One of the only states that reported no slaves in its population in 1790 was _____.

2.   _____ was the inventor of the cotton gin.

3.   The black leader of antislavery forces in Haiti who successfully overthrew French rule on that island was _____.

4.   _____ was the founder of Bethel Church in Philadelphia, the first African Methodist Church in the United States.

5.   The United States' purchase of _____ from the French made possible both the extension of cotton and sugar culture by planters of the Southern United States, and the greater entrenchment of slavery in the region.

True/False

1. In the years immediately following the Revolutionary War, there was some reason to believe that slavery would deteriorate.

2. Revolutionary activity among slaves in the Caribbean at the turn of the century had little effect on the course of United States history.

3. The federal law banning the slave trade was rigidly enforced after 1808.

4. Fearing that unruly slaves imported from Africa or the Caribbean would foment insurrection on plantations, American merchants and planters overwhelmingly supported federal nonimportation legislation.

Relevance Today

1. The decision by the Northern states to abolish slavery in the revolutionary period profoundly affected the attitudes of later residents toward slavery. Do you feel that legislation today can profoundly affect the attitudes of citizens with respect to ethnically/culturally dissimilar people. Consider the Civil Rights Act of 1964 (chapter 23), the Voting Rights of 1965 (chapter 23), or Proposition 209 in California (chapter 24) prohibiting race-specific college admission policy. To what extent can public attitudes be shaped in response to legislated policy?

2. Numerous forces conspired to check the development of schools for blacks in this time period. What influences today do you believe constitute major impediments to education for African Americans?

CHAPTER 7
BLACKS AND MANIFEST DESTINY

THEMES AND MAJOR POINTS

Although a spirit of freedom was strong on the frontier, the greater portion of those whites who moved west from the Atlantic coastal states was committed to the institution of slavery and, when possible, brought slaves with them.

African Americans were participants in the exploration and settlement of the American West as trappers, traders, guides, hunters, interpreters, explorers, wilderness fighters, scouts, gold prospectors, and missionaries.

During the War of 1812, blacks served their country as soldiers and sailors and as volunteers in civil defense activities. In the last major engagement of the war, the Battle of New Orleans, African-American soldiers occupied a position of strategic importance that helped produce a victory for the U.S. forces.

After 1815 large numbers of white settlers, many of them planters bringing their slaves from the seaboard states, moved into the Gulf region of the South to clear the rich lands and cultivate extensive crops of cotton. The wealth produced in the region caused it to be described as the Cotton Kingdom. The great profits from cotton cultivation stimulated new waves of immigration, strengthened the institution of slavery, and fed the planters' hunger for new western lands.

One of the most important single factors augmenting the western movement was the domestic slave trade. It was profitable, widespread, cruel, and brutal.

So great was the demand for slaves and the profit in providing them that the African slave trade, though outlawed by federal legislation after 1808, continued to supply the planters of the South.

KEY EVENTS

1803   Louisiana purchased.

1803–1806   Lewis and Clark expedition occurred.

1812   Louisiana entered the Union as the eighteenth state.
              War with Great Britain commenced.

1814   Treaty of Ghent signed: war concluded.

1817   Mississippi entered the Union as the twentieth state.

1819   Alabama entered the Union as the twenty-second state.

1820   Missouri Compromise; Missouri entered the Union as the
              twenty-fourth state.

CHAPTER OVERVIEW

The initial years of the nineteenth century provided citizens of the United States with ample reason for optimism. Land was cheap and plentiful, and, with the acquisition of the Louisiana Territory, farming soil seemed virtually limitless. The cost of these frontier blessings and the concomitant of white liberty and democracy, however, would be borne by the black race in America. To areas south of the Ohio River, and especially to the rich soils of the southwest territories, slave traders rushed their commodities to bolster the newly created Cotton Kingdom. Between 1812 and 1820, four slave states were added to the Union.

Expansionism had other costs. Aggressive expansionists from the western and southern states of America contributed in large measure to the outbreak of war with Great Britain in 1812. While the war was economically disastrous for the young American economy, it provided the opportunity for many blacks to obtain their freedom. As in the Revolutionary War, blacks served the United States with valor and distinction. With the conclusion of the war came an acceleration of western migration and the expansion of slavery. Prices for field hands doubled in some areas after the war, thus prompting both the expansion of America's illegal slave imports and southern calls to repeal the 1807 ban on the foreign slave trade. Clearly the emergent theories of "manifest destiny" had different connotations for blacks and whites in America.

REVIEW QUESTIONS

Chapter Content Review

1. What forces rendered resistance to the encroaching forces of slavery futile?

2. What contributions did black Americans, such as York, Edward Rose, and Pierre Bonga, make to the settlement of the American West?

3. Why did the American "warhawks" expect that war with Great Britain would advance or extend slavery?

4. What contributions did blacks make to the 1812 war effort?

5. What factors accounted for the great emigration of southerners to the West during the first third of the nineteenth century?

6. What relevance did Texas have to the lords of the Cotton Kingdom during the first half of the nineteenth century?

7.   What effect did the interstate trafficking of slaves have on antislavery sentiment in Maryland and Virginia?

8.   What impact did the 1807 ban on the importation of African slaves have on American slaving interests?

9.   For what reasons might slave owners hire out or lease their slaves?

10.   For what reason would an individual who owned no slaves hire a slave from a slaveowner instead of purchasing one?

11.   What competition did America's interstate slave traders face in the first half of the nineteenth century?

12.   Why did the states of the upper South reject calls to reopen the slave trade?

Identification Questions

You should be able to describe the following key terms, concepts, individuals, and places and explain their significance:

1.   James Beckwourth
2.   Edmonia Lewis
3.   warhawks
4.   Treaty of Ghent
5.   Manifest Destiny
6.   slave breeding

Essay Questions

1.   Despite numerous geographical and economic differences, the various parts of the South developed into an economically united section of the United States. Explain the reasons for this.

2. "The slave trader had a more profound effect on the history of the southern frontier than did the Indian trader." Defend or dispute this assertion.

SELF-TEST

Multiple-Choice

1. One of the causes of the War of 1812 was
   a. British efforts to end the slave trade.
   b. the desire of some American leaders to acquire more territory.
   c. the failure to resolve a boundary dispute between the United States and British Canada.
   d. Britain's attempt to regain American lands lost in the Revolution.

2. This was called the "very seat and center of the slave trade."
   a. Charleston
   b. Memphis
   c. the District of Columbia
   d. New Orleans

3. Which of the following represented the attempt to secure a supply of labor for work in the Cotton Kingdom?
   a. establishment of the domestic slave trade
   b. illegal importation of slaves from Africa
   c. both a and b
   d. neither a nor b

4. Which one of the following groups did not help push back the American frontier and create the slave states that entered the Union?
    a. young, adventurous people from the seaboard states
    b. young slave owners from the West Indies, Brazil, and Mexico
    c. Scotch-Irish and German immigrants from Europe

5. The blacks who served under Major Daquin in the Battle of New Orleans were
    a. from St. Domingue.
    b. loyal slaves recruited from Louisiana plantations.
    c. free blacks from New Orleans.
    d. free blacks from Maryland.

Fill-in-the-Blank

1. _____ was described as "the most intrepid and remarkable of the black explorers of the American West."

2. _____ were those members of Congress representing southern and western states that advocated war with Britain in 1812.

3. The _____ was the 1787 statute that prohibited slavery in the territory north of the Ohio River.

4. _____ was the term used to describe the argument that the area of the United States must be extended so as to make possible the development of a great "empire for liberty" in the New World.

5. Two of the wealthiest of the slave-trading firms were _____ and _____.

True/False

1. There is no record of blacks participating in the exploration of the trans-Mississippi West.

2. One of the most important factors augmenting the westward movement was the domestic slave trade.

3. Blacks served in the army but not in the navy in the War of 1812.

4. The extension of democracy was not the primary motive of the Southern expansionists.

5. Although slaves often brought higher prices when sold separately, slave owners and slave traders refused to sell family members away from each other.

Relevance Today

1. When black Americans assisted white Americans in conquering the Indians and taking their land, ironically, they were an oppressed group assisting in the exploitation of another oppressed group. Are there examples in the United States today of oppressed groups assisting in the exploitation of other oppressed groups?

2. When pioneers who were slave owners said they were committed to freedom, they meant that people like them were free to pursue self-interest, including the use of others for their benefit. Are there men and women in the United States today whose behavior indicates they share the same belief?

3. Slavery produced great wealth for cotton planters. Do you see ways of producing wealth in our country at the present time that seem to depend on the exploitation of working people? If so, who is responsible for this?

4.   Because the African slave trade supplied workers who were crucial to the creation of wealth in the Cotton Kingdom, many Americans were willing to violate the law that forbade the slave trade. Which of our country's laws are violated today by some people seeking to amass great wealth?

CHAPTER 8
THAT PECULIAR INSTITUTION

THEMES AND MAJOR POINTS

- Demand for cotton during the Industrial Revolution both increased the demand for slave workers on the frontier and intensified the repressive features of slavery in America.

- Although three-fourths of the southern families owned no slaves, slavery became the dominant influence in the political, economic, and social decisions of the South.

- Plantations constituted the greatest unit of Southern agrarian production, and, consequently, the largest planters tended to have the greatest political, economic, and social influence.

- The intense concern with stable crop production meant that many planters and farmers produced too little nutritious food to sustain a healthy lifestyle.

- Despite the common attitude that blacks lacked the requisite intelligence to be tradespeople, most southern towns depended heavily on the production of numerous black craftspeople.

- Religion for slaves constituted a source of solace and hope. Religion, in the eyes of slave owners, was a means by which control would be maintained over slaves.

- As a rule, the capriciousness of the slave system impeded the development of stable family bonds.

- Throughout the history of slavery, slaves consistently demonstrated their antipathy to the system by revolting, fleeing, or resisting in numerous ways.

KEY EVENTS

1790   Slave population of the United States was about 690,000.

1800   Gabriel Prosser led a slave insurrection in Virginia.

1822   Denmark Vesey's planned slave insurrection was thwarted in South Carolina.

1830   Slave population of the United States was about 2,100,000.

1831   Nat Turner led a slave revolt in Southampton County, Virginia.

CHAPTER OVERVIEW

In the first half of the nineteenth-century, slavery expanded throughout the South and serves as the basis for the expansion of Southern wealth and production. At the same time, slavery exerted increasing influence on the course of the South's social and political developments. As cotton cultivators, the slaves served as the essential means for accumulating wealth; as capital, they were the most important form of Southern wealth. But, this "capital" was of a peculiar nature. As human beings held in bondage and deprived of the fruits of their labor, the slave-capital required careful motivation and supervision. From these circumstances emerged the essentials of a "peculiar" institution and the peculiar Southern society of the Antebellum Period.

Rooted in agrarianism and the expansion of its staples (cotton, rice, tobacco, and sugar cane), Southern society was led by the wealthy planter class. Comprising less than 2 percent of the white families, planters nevertheless exerted dominant influence over the course of Southern economics, politics, and culture. Of primary concern to the planters and lesser slaveholders of the South was the preservation of the status quo. To control the slaves and to induce them to produce bounteous crops, rigid laws and systems of control were devised. The slave codes, community patrols, religious indoctrination, threats, and forms of torture were essential elements of the peculiar institution. Not surprisingly, insurrection was the greatest of the fears of Southern white citizenry. Although only 25 percent of these people owned slaves, all citizens had an abiding interest in preserving the slave system.

Black resistance to slavery was both persistent and omnipresent in the South. Whether simply breaking a tool or fleeing captivity, the slaves never fully accepted their status. Through song, stories, dance, religion, and familial ties, slaves created for themselves a meaningful community in which their dignity was affirmed.

REVIEW QUESTIONS

Chapter Content Review

1.   What was the size of the slave population of the United States on the eve of the Civil War? What was the size of the Southern white population?

2.   How did slavery shape the social structure of the South and dominate the political and economic thinking of Southerners?

3.   For what purposes were the slave codes created? What did they prohibit?

4.   By what means were slave codes enforced?

5.   How many acres of cotton could a single slave typically plant, cultivate, and harvest in a single year?

6. Why were slaves directed by an overseer more likely to receive crueler treatment than slaves under the direction of the plantation owner?

7. How many slaves lived in urban communities in 1850? In what type of work were they engaged?

8. In what types of recreational activities did plantation slaves frequently engage?

9. Why did slave owners frequently demand slave attendance at Christian services held at white churches?

10. Why did many planters fear slave piety?

11. What impact did the illegal schools for Southern blacks have after the Civil War?

12. What obstacles prevented slaves from forming stable family units?

13. What percentage of the slave population was visibly mulatto in 1850?

14. What types of legal restrictions prevented cruel or inhuman treatment toward slaves?

15. What form of Negro resistance to slavery did white communities fear most?

Identification Questions

You should be able to describe the following key terms, concepts, individuals, and places and explain their significance:

1. slave codes
2. patrols
3. vigilance committees
4. field hand
5. house servant
6. Henry Blair
7. Benjamin Montgomery
8. John Canoe celebration
9. Gabriel Prosser
10. Denmark Vesey
11. Nat Turner

Essay Questions

1. If you had to make the unenviable choice of living as a field hand (slave) or a house servant (slave), which would it be? Why? What advantages/disadvantages do you see in each?

2. Commonly heard among the planter class were accusations that their slaves were guilty of delinquency, thievery, sloth, and aversion to "civilizing" tendencies. What aspects of slave life may have contributed to the formulation of these accusations?

SELF-TEST

Multiple-Choice

1. In 1860, three-fourths of the white people of the South
   a. owned twenty or more slaves.
   b. had neither slaves nor an immediate economic interest in the maintenance of slavery.
   c. were operators of large plantations.
   d. favored the immediate abolition of slavery.

2. Slave codes expressed the point of view that
   a. slaves were not persons but property.
   b. laws should protect the ownership of slave property.
   c. whites should be protected against possible slave rebellion.
   d. all of the above.

3. It was generally believed that
   a. one slave was required for the cultivation of three acres of cotton.
   b. each slave should be given a specific work assignment or task each day.
   c. house servants were more valuable than field hands.
   d. slaves should never be exposed to any form of religious activity.

4. All of the following men led slave rebellions which terrified Southern communities except
   a. Gabriel Prosser
   b. Denmark Vesey
   c. Nat Turner
   d. John Canoe

5.   Which of the following necessities did the average slave receive?
    a.   adequate footwear and clothing
    b.   healthy and sufficient food
    c.   comfortable shelter
    d.   none of the above

Fill-in-the-Blank

1.   Although a distinct minority in Southern society, the
    _____ were that class that exercised a disproportionate
    amount of influence.

2.   The _____ was an adoption of the militia in the South
    used to maintain slavery. It enforced the slave codes in
    communities.

3.   Plantation slaves labored generally under the "task" or "gang"
    system. Under which did the majority work? _____

4.   _____ was one of the major religious denominations in
    the antebellum lower South that had the greatest influence on
    plantation slaves.

True/False

1.   A majority of Southern whites owned slaves.

2.   Slave owners generally selected their overseers from the
    slaveholding class.

3.   Despite legal restrictions, some slaves were taught to read and
    write.

4.   The Southern churches served as vehicles for maintaining slavery.

5.   As a rule, field hands tended to view themselves as socially superior to house slaves.

6.   Despite their status as chattel, slaves enjoyed abundant opportunities for recreation.

Relevance Today

1.   Franklin and Moss hold that "the strong individualism that was bred on the frontier plantation and the planter's self-conception as the source of law and justice had the effect of discouraging conformity to statutes even when they were passed in the interest of the plantation system." Do you feel that Americans today possess such strong individualism that they will typically ignore or disregard laws enacted for their own interests? Explain.

2.   Interracial class distinctions have existed for at least 150 years: "House servants were even anxious to 'work' their children into the more desirable situation and to marry them off to the children of other house servants." In African-American communities today, what are the chief determinants of social status: (a) for adults and (b) for teenagers? To what extent does desire for status interfere with building and sustaining secure and vibrant communities?

3.   "Any understanding of reactions to slave status must be approached with the realization that the slave at times was possessed of a dual personality and could be one person at one time and quite a different person at another." Do you think that African Americans have dual personalities today? If you feel that it is true, to what extent do you feel that dual personalities give rise to confusion and misunderstanding among members of different ethnic or racial groups?

CHAPTER 9
QUASI-FREE BLACKS

THEMES AND MAJOR POINTS

From the end of the Revolutionary War to the start of the Civil War, the number of free blacks grew steadily, yet the situation of free blacks, wherever they lived, was precarious. By the start of the Civil War, their status had declined to the point that the distinction between free and slave blacks was hardly discernible.

To the best of their ability and with limited success, free blacks sought economic independence, struggled to create stable families, provided organized recreational activities for their communities, established fraternal and benevolent organizations as well as independent churches and denominations, and, in a variety of ways, sought to create and expand educational opportunities for themselves and their children.

The achievements and struggles of the free black community were reflected in the black newspapers established during this period and in the books written by men and women who were a part of that community.

In response to the accelerating violence against them in the North and West, free African Americans held regular meetings or conventions to devise ways of improving their situation and to protest mistreatment.

Though some free blacks explored options for removal to other parts of the world as an alternative to their difficult lives in the United States, generally there was widespread opposition to colonization schemes throughout the free black community.

KEY EVENTS

1790   There were 59,000 free blacks in the United States.

1810   Maryland repealed the right of black suffrage.

1817   American Colonization Society was formed

1826   First blacks graduated from American colleges.

1827   *Freedman's Journal*, the first African-American newspaper was
       published.

1830   There were 319,000 free blacks in the United States.

1834   Tennessee repealed black suffrage laws.
       African Methodist Episcopal Church began publishing *The
       Christian Herald*.

1853   The National Council of Colored People established.

1860   There were 488,000 free blacks in the United States.

CHAPTER OVERVIEW

One peculiarity of the slave societies in the antebellum South was
the existence of "free blacks." Neither slave nor free, these descendants of
manumitted people and exindentures lived at the fringe of Southern
society (except perhaps in the states of Maryland and Virginia) and lived
as inconspicuously as possible. Because their status as nonslaves
contradicted the cultural distinction of whites/free and blacks/slave,
Southern white legislatures imposed increasingly rigid restrictions on the
quasi-free blacks to minimize the impact their "freedom" might have on
their enslaved brethren.

North of the Mason-Dixon line, where slavery had been abolished, free blacks also faced innumerable obstacles in securing for themselves the blessings conferred upon independent citizens. Usually denied political and social rights in the states and communities where they dwelled, and not infrequently the victims of rigid segregation and violent attacks, Northern blacks responded by creating independent institutions: churches, newspapers, businesses, and social service networks which catered to their interests.

Whether from the North or the South, free blacks had few opportunities to enjoy the lands of the American West. Western states often prohibited black settlement within their borders. Free blacks who did settle west of the Appalachian Mountains faced the hostility of white communities, rampant discrimination, and requisite segregation. Not suprisingly, no small number of free blacks in the Antebellum Period found the notion of colonization in Africa appealing.

REVIEW QUESTIONS

Chapter Content Review

1. For what reasons did Southern masters manumit their slaves?

2. What factors, other than manumission, account for the increase in the number of free blacks in the South?

3. In what areas of the country were free blacks concentrated on the eve of the Civil War?

4. Why was the existence of free blacks in the South so precarious?

5. What economic and legal restrictions were imposed on the free blacks in the South?

6. What became of black suffrage in America after the Revolutionary Era?

7. What impediments prevented free black tradespeople from enjoying economic liberty?

8. What accounted for the growth of black fraternal and benevolent institutions in urban centers prior to the Civil War?

9. What happened to the black Methodist and Baptist churches between 1820 and 1860?

10. How common was public education for blacks in the Midwest prior to the Civil War?

11. What institutions of higher learning were created for blacks in the antebellum years?

12. Despite mob violence, rampant discrimination, and mandated segregation, free blacks in the North had a great advantage over Southern free blacks. Explain.

13. Where did the colonization approach to the "Negro problem" originate and what was Paul Cuffe's contribution to it?

14. For what reasons did the American Colonization Society fail?

Identification Questions

You should be able to describe the following key terms, concepts, individuals, and places and explain their significance:

1. Cyprian Ricard
2. Solomon Humphries
3. placage

4. *The Christian Herald*
5. Phoenix Societies
6. George Moses Horton
7. William Wells Brown
8. *Freedom's Journal*
9. *North Star*
10. National Council of Colored People

Essay Questions

1. Despite their status as legally free, "free" blacks were no better than bondsmen. Assess the validity of this assertion.

2. The history of the colonization movement is filled with examples of black disharmony. Explain why emigration from America was simultaneously applauded and scorned by different black groups within the United States.

SELF-TEST

Multiple-Choice

1. Census figures reveal that this state had a larger population of free blacks than any other.
   a. Virginia
   b. Maryland
   c. Pennsylvania
   d. New York

2. Despite the organized effort to colonize free blacks, about only _____ migrated.
   a. 1,420
   b. 30,000
   c. 10,000
   d. 15,000

3. The first black newspaper published in the United States was
   a. *Freedom's Journal.*
   b. *North Star.*
   c. *Colored Man's Journal.*
   d. *Anglo-African.*

4. The first American black to write a play and a novel was
   a. William Wells Brown.
   b. John Russwurm.
   c. Frederick Douglass.
   d. James McCune Smith.

5. Most of the free blacks for whom the Colonization Society provided money to leave the United States went to
   a. Canada.
   b. Mexico.
   c. Liberia.
   d. South America.

Fill-in-the-Blank

1. _____ was the legal status of children born to free mothers.

2. The _____ was the name of the newspaper first published by Frederick Douglass in 1847.

3. The _____ was an organization formed for the purpose of commencing the colonization of American blacks in Africa.

4. In 1828, the free black who owned the largest number of slaves in the South was _____.

5. _____ and _____ were whites who noted in their writings how badly mistreated free blacks were in the North and West.

True/False

1. Some slaves were able to gain their freedom through self-purchase.

2. Manumission carried with it civil and political rights as well as legal freedom.

3. Free blacks hated slavery so much they refused to become _____ slaveholders.

4. Racial animosity in the North forced blacks in that section to totally support colonization.

5. One reason the number of free blacks grew was that masters manumitted their slaves in large numbers.

Relevance Today

1. During this period, free blacks established newspapers for their communities because white newspapers seldom printed positive information about blacks and their communities. The information white newspapers did print about blacks was usually hostile, demeaning, and negative. Why do you think bye African-American owned and run newspapers whose circulation is primarily in the African-American community exist today?

2. Free blacks' greatest struggles were to gain economic independence and to create stable families. Why are so many African-American families facing the same struggles today? Are there some African Americans today for whom these struggles are no longer major concerns?

3. Though most free blacks opposed colonization schemes to remove them from the United States, some thought colonization was a good idea. Are there attitudes and behaviors in the African-American community today indicating that some blacks think removal to another part of the world would solve their problems? Do you think that colonization is the answer to the present-day problems of African Americans?

4. Free blacks held meetings to devise ways of improving their situation and to protest mistreatment. Identify groups of African Americans who do the same things today in the effort to resolve their problems. Indicate which groups seem to be effective and which groups ineffective.

CHAPTER 10
SLAVERY AND INTERSECTIONAL STRIFE

THEMES AND MAJOR POINTS

- The antislavery movement in the United States grew from the religious, humanitarian, and political beliefs and ideals of the late eighteenth century.

- Countenancing of violence by abolitionists caused many law-abiding citizens to oppose them entirely.

- The antislavery leaders in the West emerged from both the frontier seminary colleges and the ranks of Southerners that had moved west because of the hostility in the South toward reform.

- The Underground Railroad both intensified the strife between North and South and emphasized the determination of abolitionists to destroy slavery.

- In the decade before the Civil War, proslavery leaders resolved to keep the institution of slavery inviolate by destroying every vestige of thought that was at variance with it.

- The discovery of gold in California, coupled with the rapid settling of Mexican Cession lands, moved the slave question into the chambers of Congress; there, the Compromise of 1850 was fashioned.

- After John Brown's raid, capture, and martyrdom, Southern militias formed and prepared for war.

- Ultimately, it was the question of slavery that aggravated sectional tensions, intensified the reform crusade, led to the rise of the Republican Party in 1860, and convinced Southerners of the need for secession.

KEY EVENTS

1820   Congress defused sectional tensions by enacting the Missouri Compromise.

1821   The Genius of Universal Emancipation first published.

1829   David Walker's Appeal published.

1831   The Liberator first published.
New England Antislavery Society formed.

1840   Liberty Party formed.

1847   Frederick Douglass elected president of the New England Anti-Slavery Society.

1850   Slave trade in the District of Columbia is abolished.
Fugitive Slave Act enacted.

1852   *Uncle Tom's Cabin* first published.

1854   Kansas-Nebraska Act became law.
Republican Party formed.

1857   *Dred Scott v. Sanford* decision declared the Missouri Compromise unconstitutional.

1859   John Brown conducted raid on Harper's Ferry.

1860   Republican Abraham Lincoln elected president.

CHAPTER OVERVIEW

Costly though the War of 1812 was, it nevertheless contributed briefly to the formation of national unity and greater political cooperation among the states of the North and South, yet the essential differences between the increasingly reformist and industrial North and the slave-dependent agrarian South created a wedge with the potential to divide the sections permanently. In 1819, two powerful American values, antislavery and expansionism, converged and clashed in the congressional deliberations over the fate of Missouri, which had sought admission to the Union as the twelfth slave state. Compromise was the solution to the sectional breach in 1820, but the seeds of mutual distrust had been sown.

Prior to the 1820s, religious antislavery and economic considerations had pressured slave owners to improve the conditions of slavery, manumit slaves, or support the colonization movement. Gradually, however, the antislavery movement became increasingly strident and intolerant of the "peculiar" institution and those who maintained it. Abolitionists such as David Walker, William Lloyd Garrison, Frederick Douglass, and Theodore Weld infuriated white Southerners with their publications. In response, some white Southerners began to fashion an ideological defense of slavery and the Southern way of life. Moreover, as the abolitionist attacks increased, white Southerners closed ranks and flexed their political muscle. In 1836, Southern congressmen were able to impose the "gag rule" in Congress, preventing the reading of antislavery petitions sent to the House of Representatives. In the 1840s, Southern politicians successfully promoted the future expansion of slavery by securing the annexation of Texas and by winning the Mexican Cession lands via war.

Unlike the war of 1812, the Mexican War divided Northerners and Southerners and put an end to the national consensus regarding American expansionism. To Northerners, expansionism had become synonymous with extending and perpetuating chattel slavery, and this they wouldn't countenance. To Southerners, the opportunity to cultivate soils in the West with the aid of their human property became a prerequisite for their continuation in the Union. Throughout the 1850s, this conflict intensified. The Compromise of 1850, which was crafted by congressional leaders to preserve national unity, proved completely inadequate to the task of resolving what had become a divisive, emotional, and moral issue to a majority of Americans. Popular sovereignty applied in Kansas, a strengthened fugitive slave law, and the Supreme Court's 1857 Dred Scott decision all exacerbated the sectional tensions they were intended to quell.

Finally in 1859 an abolitionist by the name of John Brown demonstrated to the South how their peculiar institution might be destroyed, and shortly thereafter the sword replaced both the pen and politics as the means for resolving the sectional conflict.

REVIEW QUESTIONS

Chapter Content Review

1. Which individuals initiated radical abolitionism in America?

2. How did the abolitionism of David Walker and William Lloyd Garrison differ?

3. With what other reform movements of the early eighteenth century was militant antislavery associated?

4. How did James Birney and Theodore Weld advance the cause of antislavery?

5. Why did Garrison split the American Anti-Slavery Society in 1839?

6. How did the Liberty Party originate?

7. Which abolitionist tactic engendered the greatest opposition to abolitionism in America?

8. How active were blacks in the national antislavery organizations?

9. Why was Frederick Douglass so important to the antislavery movement?

10. Why was the Underground Railroad such a threat to sectional harmony after 1830?

11. Approximately how many slaves escaped via the Underground Railroad between 1810 and 1850?

12. What events in the early 1820s convinced the residents of the South that they had to give more attention to the defense of slavery?

13. Other than writing pamphlets, in what other activities did Southern communities engage to limit abolitionism?

14. What groups in America were steadfast against the compromise measures of 1850?

15. In what way did the Kansas-Nebraska Act of 1854 doom the Compromise of 1850?

16. What impact did the Dred Scott decision have on the antislavery movement?

17. What impact did John Brown's raid on Harper's Ferry have on the South?

18. Why was the South unalterably opposed to the Republican Party?

Identification Questions

You should be able to describe the following key terms, concepts, individuals, and places and explain their significance:

1. David Walker
2. Benjamin Lundy
3. William Lloyd Garrison
4. Charles Finney
5. Oberlin College
6. Lewis Tappan
7. American and Foreign Anti-Slavery Society
8. Elijah Lovejoy
9. gag rule
10. Joshua Giddings
11. Samuel Cornish
12. *Freedom's Journal*
13. Harriet Tubman
14. John Fairfield
15. Harriet Beecher Stowe
16. Kansas-Nebraska Act
17. John Brown

Essay Questions

1. What religious, ideological, economic, and cultural arguments were made against slavery in America?

2. What arguments did the defenders of slavery make to justify the institution?

3.   The "Negro problem" was undoubtedly the single greatest issue confronting all Americans from 1812 to 1850. Explain what this "problem" involved and why it created such tension.

SELF-TEST

Multiple-Choice

1.   Which part of the Compromise of 1850 did the South find absolutely essential?
       a.   The admission of California as a free state.
       b.   The provision that certain territories be organized without mention of slavery (i.e., organized according to popular sovereignty).
       c.   A stringent fugitive slave law.
       d.   The abolition of the slave trade in the District of Columbia.

2.   Which of the following arguments was not part of the Southern defense of slavery?
       a.   Black people were inferior and destined for a subordinate position in society.
       b.   The Bible sanctioned slavery.
       c.   Slavery was unprofitable: if let alone it would rapidly fade out.
       d.   Slave labor was an economic necessity to the South.

3.   The election of 1860 brought to the presidency
       a.   one who advocated reopening the African slave trade.
       b.   an opponent of the further extension of slavery.
       c.   a man highly acceptable to Southerners.
       d.   a militant abolitionist.

4. Approximately how many men and women escaped from slavery between 1810 and 1850?
   a. 10,000
   b. 30,000
   c. 100,000
   d. 500,000

5. All of the following people assisted slaves in achieving liberation through the Underground Railroad except
   a. John Fairfield.
   b. Elijah Anderson.
   c. Levi Coffin.
   d. Dred Scott.

Fill-in-the-Blank

1. The name given to the action of the House of Representatives that, from 1836 to 1845, denied Americans the right of petition was the

   _____.

2. The _____ was an organized effort to undermine slavery by assisting runaway slaves escaping from the South.

3. Militant abolitionists were unalterably opposed to _____ as an approach to the "Negro problem." They felt that, rather than an approach to abolishing slavery, it was a means of draining off the free black population to make slavery more secure.

4. _____ was the best known of all black abolitionists. He published the *North Star,* lectured throughout the North and England, and worked actively in the Underground Railroad.

5. _____ was an outstanding black journalist who not only established the first black newspaper, *Freedom's Journal,* but also published and edited the *Weekly Advocate.*

True/False

1. Militant abolitionists supported the idea of financial compensation to owners of freed slaves.

2. Militant abolitionists were, on the whole, opposed to colonization.

3. Northern black men spoke out in favor of emancipation but were not permitted to support it in print.

4. Lincoln won the election of 1860 primarily because of his substantial electoral vote from the South.

5. Blacks in the North were reluctant to support Garrison or any other abolitionist.

Relevance Today

1. The abolitionists took stances, public and private (such as aiding and abetting the Underground Railroad), that led to both threats and crimes against them. What do you value so intensely that you would willingly face the same dangers as the abolitionists?

2. The institution of slavery did more than breed a culture of violence in the South. It also bred a tendency toward duplicity and self-delusion. Perhaps in denial, in order to assuage their own fears of revolt, Southerners frequently claimed that their slaves were content with their lot. In another moment, they decried their ungrateful slaves who had fled. Southerners claimed blacks couldn't achieve literacy or become skilled tradespeople, yet tens of thousands did learn and create. In contemporary terminology,

Southern communities were highly dysfunctional societies. Do you feel that American leaders and role models—politicians, teachers, ministers, filmmakers, professional athletes, and parents—black or not, discredit themselves, undermine their own authority, and engender dysfunctional cultures in the United States when thy conceal or distort the truth? Do you feel that citizens in general would be better served if more relationships were based on truthfulness?

3. Southerners engaged in acts of massive resistance to federal law by seizing antislavery newspapers from post offices; after this, Southern postmasters decided not to deliver antislavery mail. Under what circumstances do you feel that First Amendment liberties (e.g., right to free speech and free press) can be abridged by the will of a community? Is resistance to federal law ever justified? Is lawbreaking in general an entrenched part of American culture?

CHAPTER 11
THE CIVIL WAR

THEMES AND MAJOR POINTS

During the early phases of the Civil War, President Abraham Lincoln and the federal government moved cautiously in regard to blacks and their concerns. Significantly, not until 1862 were blacks allowed to serve in the Union military forces.

The policy of the Lincoln administration on the emancipation of slaves evolved slowly, culminating in President Lincoln's Emancipation Proclamation, which took effect on January 1, 1863.

At the start of the Civil War, white Southerners' fears about the conduct of their slaves proved to be well founded. As slaves became aware that in this war their freedom was at stake, many deserted or were unmanageable. One of the ironies of the war was the confederate states' dependence on black labor to sustain their war machine. In the closing days of the Civil War, the South even recruited black soldiers.

When blacks were permitted finally to enlist in the Union army, they did so with alacrity and enthusiasm. Their service contributed greatly to the victory of the Union forces in this country's second great war for freedom.

The defeat of the South was a victory for the North, for American blacks, and, paradoxically, for the South.

KEY EVENTS

1861   (February) South Carolina, Mississippi, Florida, Alabama, Georgia, and Louisiana seceded from the Union. They convened and adopted a provisional constitution for the Confederate States of America.
(March) Lincoln was inaugurated.
(April) Civil War began as Fort Sumter was taken by South Carolina.
(May) Texas, Arkansas, Tennessee, Virginia, and North Carolina seceded.

1862   (April) Slaves emancipated in the District of Columbia.
(July) South Carolina "Negro Regiment" activated.
(September) Preliminary Emancipation Proclamation issued.

1863   (January) Emancipation Proclamation issued.
(July) Union troops defeated Confederates at Gettysburg.

1864   Sherman's March to the Sea occurred.

1865   General Robert E. Lee surrendered at Appomattox; Civil War ended.

CHAPTER OVERVIEW

The election of Republican Abraham Lincoln in November 1860 led directly to the disintegration of the union and civil war. After Lincoln's condemnation of the Southern insurrectionists and his call to arms, thousands of Northern black men sought to enlist to serve the cause of liberation. Their service, however, was spurned. The aim of the war, averred Mr. Lincoln, was to preserve the Union, not to destroy slavery. If blacks were permitted to enlist, then a majority of voters from the border states still in the Union—Maryland, Missouri, Delaware, and Kentucky, as well as anti-abolitionists in the North—might perceive abolitionism to be the Northern war aim. The support or neutrality of these people the Union could ill afford to lose, yet at the same time the Union could not destroy the Confederacy without the contributions of African Americans. Only gradually did Lincoln appear to grasp this, and only gradually did emancipation become fully intertwined with preservation of the Union as the Northern war objective.

The millions of Southern slaves grasped immediately that the war was about slavery and its eradication. Despite vacillating and ambiguous Union racial policies, they escaped by the thousands and quickly demonstrated their value to the Union. Each slave lost to the South both weakened the Confederacy and potentially strengthened the forces of the Union. Union generals such as Benjamin Butler, Davis Hunter, and Rufus Saxton understood this and exploited the potential of both "contrabands" and free blacks, who were permitted, at the end of 1862, to enlist in "Negro regiments." By the end of the war, nearly a million escaped slaves had served the causes of the Union and freedom. Approximately 180,000 black men served as soldiers for the Union. Of that number, nearly 40,000 perished.

As a necessary wartime measure, President Lincoln issued the Emancipation Proclamation on January 1, 1863. This not only induced slave escapes and black recruitment, but it also confirmed the revolutionary social dimension of the Civil War. At stake after January 1863 was the destruction of plantation oligarchy and the system of rigid black oppression upon which it was based. At stake for African Americans were the blessings of liberty.

This liberty, however, proved elusive to black Americans. Despite the enormity of their war contributions, and incontrovertible proof of their valor and sacrifice, black troops faced discrimination in pay, duties, and opportunity. Their families suffered countless acts of discrimination and deprivation. Promises of just treatment were repeatedly made and broken by agents of the victorious Union government.

REVIEW QUESTIONS

Chapter Content Review

1. Why was Lincoln unable to profess in 1861 that the government's objective in fighting the war was to eliminate slavery?

2. What prevented blacks from enlisting in the Union forces at the start of the war?

3. Who determined the policy for dealing with runaway slaves in the early years of the war?

4. What circumstances contributed to the appalling conditions of the camps for former slaves during the war?

5. Who was responsible for the many initial efforts in black education during the Civil War?

6. From what part of the country were the first black regiments drawn?

7. For what reasons were white Northern laborers particularly upset by the government's policies during the Civil War?

8. By what route did Lincoln attempt to emancipate the slaves of the border states during the Civil War? Why was he unsuccessful?

9. What was the reaction of the "Peace Democrats" to the Emancipation Proclamation?

10. Explain how the Emancipation Proclamation affected the slaves of America?

11. What military and diplomatic benefits did the United States derive from issuing the Emancipation Proclamation?

12. In what ways was the presence of slaves in the Confederacy a source of grave concern for whites?

13. How did the advance of Union troops affect slave behavior?

14. What types of contributions did slaves make to the Confederate war effort?

15. What positions did Jefferson Davis and Robert E. Lee take on the enlistment of slaves?

16. Approximately how many blacks served in the Union army during the Civil War?

17. Why was the mortality for black Union troops significantly higher than the rate for whites?

18. In what way was the Confederate surrender of 1865 a victory for the South?

Identification Questions

You should be able to describe the following key terms, concepts, individuals, and places, and explain their significance:

1. Benjamin F. Butler
2. "contraband of war"
3. American Missionary Association
4. New York draft riots
5. Emancipation Proclamation
6. "running the Negroes"
7. Fifty-Fourth Massachusetts Regiment
8. Robert G. Shaw
9. Fort Pillow affair

Essay Questions

1. While Lincoln is viewed by many as being the "Great Emancipator," he was greatly despised by abolitionists across the nation from 1861 to 1865. Explain why.

2. Why did popular prejudices toward blacks frequently collapse during the Civil War?

SELF-TEST

Multiple-Choice

1. Abraham Lincoln
   a. favored total and immediate emancipation of slaves.
   b. supported unconditional abolition without compensation to owners.
   c. wanted gradual emancipation with compensation to owners.
   d. opposed the idea of colonization of freed slaves outside the United States.

2. The Emancipation Proclamation
   a. represented the first official action taken with regard to slaves.
   b. liberated slaves in all slaveholding states.
   c. was enthusiastically received by Northern whites.
   d. was justified as "a fit and necessary war measure."

3. When black men first offered their service as soldiers to the Union, they
   a. were permitted to enlist, but their pay was less than that of whites.
   b. had to sign up for the duration of the war.
   c. were rejected.
   d. were accepted, but assigned to all black units.

4. One of the greatest anxieties of the South at the beginning of the war was
    a. President Lincoln's commitment to destroying slavery.
    b. the fighting ability of the black units of the Union army.
    c. how to use blacks effectively in the Confederate military forces.
    d. how the slaves would behave.

5. During the Civil War, the South used slaves in all of the following ways except
    a. on farms.
    b. in factories.
    c. mining coal.
    d. as military scouts and sharpshooters.

Fill-in-the-Blank

1. Four slave states remained loyal to the Union after 1861—Kentucky, Delaware, Missouri, and _____.

2. The _____ passed by Congress in 1861 was the first official step taken to provide "uniform treatment" for fugitives who had taken refuge behind Union lines.

3. _____ was the high-ranking Union officer who activated the short-lived "First South Carolina Volunteer Regiment" in 1862.

4. _____ This military unit served a year without pay rather than accept the discriminatory wages at first paid to black soldiers.

5.	_____ issued the order that, for every Union soldier killed in violation of the laws of war, a Rebel soldier would be put to death and that, for every Union soldier enslaved, a Rebel soldier would be placed at hard labor.

True/False

1.	Lincoln felt that the war was justified as a means of preserving the Union.

2.	Hardly a battle was fought after 1864 in which some black Union troops did not meet the enemy.

3.	From the beginning, black soldiers received the same treatment their white counterparts received.

4.	The end of the Civil War was the beginning of a new era in the history of the United States.

5.	The white workers of the North eagerly volunteered for service in the Union army and strongly urged the emancipation of the slaves.

Relevance Today

1.	Ironically, while white Southerners fought during the Civil War to keep blacks enslaved, arguing they were an inferior people, slave labor was crucial in keeping the Confederacy functioning, on the domestic front and the battlefield. Give examples of racial and ethnic groups today in the United States which are denigrated and mistreated while they are making major contributions to the well-being of this country.

2. After blacks were permitted to enter the Union army, they did so with enthusiasm and contributed to the Union victory. Did this establish a tradition that explains why significant numbers of African Americans choose to serve in the U.S. Armed Forces today?

3. Franklin and Moss argue that the defeat of the South was a victory for the South, even though the Confederacy lost. Would most white southerners today agree or disagree with this statement? Would most black southerners today agree or disagree with this statement?

4. President Abraham Lincoln moved cautiously toward support of abolition and to permit blacks to join the Union forces, yet his persistence eventually produced a Union victory that destroyed slavery. Should African Americans today view Lincoln as one of their heroes or not?

CHAPTER 12
THE EFFORT TO ATTAIN PEACE

THEMES AND MAJOR POINTS

- Reconstruction was essentially a national, not merely a sectional or racial, problem.

- Massive wartime economic expansion and expenditures, coupled with the political chaos that followed the war, created environments highly susceptible to corruption.

- Johnsonian Reconstruction was repudiated by a coalition of moderate and radical Republicans and their industrial and vengeful allies.

- Working in communities where they encountered great hostility from local whites, the officers of the Freedmen's Bureau provided medical and material relief, mediation between former slave and employers, minor courts, and schooling for former slaves of all ages and both genders.

- Independent black churches were established after the Civil War, and these gave African Americans an opportunity to develop leadership skills for the future.

- The black codes constituted the South's effort to address the difficulties stemming from war devastation and emancipation. The Freedmen's Bureau constituted the federal government's response to war devastation and emancipation.

- One of the greatest failures of Reconstitution involved the failure of state governments to make widespread improvement in the economic conditions confronting the vast number of freedmen.

- Following the Civil War, the South struggled to re-establish its agrarian economy, while the North and the West responded to the quickening pace of living ushered in by industrialization.

- During Reconstruction, the South, as well as the North, was subject to the most dynamic political and economic currents that had ever stirred the nation.

- Although Reconstruction in the South ultimately laid some foundations for more democratic living in the future, in the short range it left the former slaves with no alternatives but to submit to their old masters and participate in a system of restored white supremacy.

<u>KEY EVENTS</u>

1863   Lincoln's Ten Percent Plan announced.

1864   Congress enacted the Wade-Davis Bill.

1865   Freedmen's Bureau established.
Thirteenth Amendment enacted.

1867   Reconstruction Act of 1867 enacted.
Congressional Reconstruction commenced.

1868   Fourteenth Amendment ratified.

1870   Fifteenth Amendment ratified.

CHAPTER OVERVIEW

The Civil War concluded in the spring of 1865. The ravages of that war would be felt well into the twentieth century. Millions of people in the war-torn South were destitute, homeless, and hungry. The productive capacity of the region declined to a fraction of its 1860 level. Southern property losses ran well into the billions. There remained little Southern banking of which to speak. Most troubling, however, was the labor transformation of the South. The Civil War destroyed the basis of the Southern labor system by eradicating chattel slavery. Emancipation also threw Southern social institutions into complete disarray. Politically, the war shattered the rule of the planter oligarchs and left the South in chaos. Finally, the war unleashed the forces of industrial capitalism in the North and paved the way for the domination of the nation by Northern capitalists and their Republican allies.

Within this context, the program of Abraham Lincoln and then, after his murder, that of this successor, Andrew Johnson, were tried. Lincoln's plan encouraged rapid Southern restoration to the Union, and Johnson accepted the framework of Lincoln's plan. However, after Johnson acquiesced in both the re-empowerment of the secessionist leaders and the enactment of state black codes, Congress repudiated presidential Reconstruction and imposed its own plan. Led by the Radical Republicans, Congress passed and secured (over Johnson's vetoes) the Civil Rights Act of 1866, an extension and expansion of the Freedmen's Bureau, the Reconstruction Act of 1867, and eventually the Fourteenth and Fifteenth Amendments to the Constitution.

After 1867, the endeavors of the Southern state legislatures to establish peace and prosperity were genuine but not often successful. These "radical" state legislatures were composed primarily of Southern unionists, Northern "carpetbaggers," and African Americans. They approved large expenditures to boost internal improvements, rebuild war-damaged areas, and further public education. These state governments amply demonstrated the abilities of African Americans to hold public office responsibly and to serve their constituents effectively. Moreover, black politicians from the South were sent to the United States House of Representatives and the Senate for the first time in American history. In sum, Radical Reconstruction provided the context within which black Americans could participate in and benefit from the democratic order of America.

REVIEW QUESTIONS

Chapter Content Review

1. What factors contributed to the rapid pace of Northern industrialization during the war?

2. What immediate economic problems confronted the South after the Civil War?

3. What dangers existed in reuniting the Southern states to the Union?

4. What barriers prevented the nation from resolving a multitude of problems in 1865?

5. What were the provisions of President Andrew Johnson's Reconstruction plans?

6. What groups merged in 1865 to oppose Johnsonian Reconstruction? What motivated the opposition of each group?

7. What actions taken by President Andrew Johnson in 1866 won him the bitter enmity of Congress?

8. What were the functions of the Freedmen's Bureau? Why did white Southerners and white Northerners object to its existence?

9. In what area did the Freedmen's Bureau have the greatest success?

10. Why was the growth of black churches so important to both Reconstruction and the future of black institutions?

11. What prevented the former slaves from achieving enduring economic freedom in the South?

12. What factors militated against cooperation between black and white urban workers in the United States after the Civil War?

13. What obstacles prevented blacks from achieving many successes in starting businesses after the Civil War?

14. What type of blacks typically served in the state legislatures of the South during Reconstruction?

15. What improvements were made in the Southern state governments during the Reconstruction?

16. What type of power did black legislators usually wield in the Southern state assemblies after the Civil War?

17. What issues were most significant to the American public and American politicians after 1870?

18. Why did the nation's industrialists seek the end of Reconstruction after 1870?

19. How did Reconstruction lay the foundation for more democratic living in the South? What did the failure of Reconstruction to provide economic security for the former slaves ultimately mean to the South?

Identification Questions

You should be able to describe the following key terms, concepts, individuals, and places and explain their significance:

1. Lincoln's Ten Percent Plan
2. Wade-Davis Bill
3. black codes
4. Thaddeus Stevens
5. Freedmen's Bureau
6. Reconstruction Act of 1867
7. Fourteenth Amendment
8. Oliver O. Howard
9. Southern Homestead Act of 1866
10. Freedmen's Bank
11. Hiram Revels
12. Blanche K. Bruce
13. Fifteenth Amendment

Essay Questions

1. In what ways did the political turmoil of the post–Civil War years adversely affect the freedmen?

2. In what ways were the late nineteenth-century American industrialists responsible for the failure of the former slaves to win economic independence in the South?

SELF-TEST

Multiple-Choice

1. With regard to former slaves, the Freedmen's Bureau did all of the following except
    a. provide them all with forty acres of land and a mule.
    b. furnish supplies and medical service.
    c. supervise work contracts between former slaves and employers.
    d. establish schools.

2. An early blunder committed by the South was the
    a. repeal of the black codes.
    b. creation of the Freedmen's Bureau.
    c. rejection of the Fourteenth Amendment.
    d. strong opposition to President Johnson's policies.

3. Lincoln's "Ten Percent Plan"
    a. granted citizenship to 10 percent of the former slaves.
    b. was designed to restore control in the South to high former Confederate officeholders.
    c. had the same provisions as the Wade-Davis Bill.
    d. offered amnesty to many Southerners.

4. Northern industrialization accelerated during the Civil War because of each of the following factors except
    a. cheap cotton imported from the South.
    b. protective tariff legislation.
    c. expansion of the railroads for expanding and linking markets.
    d. many new technological developments.

5. Which of the following statements about Johnsonian Reconstruction is false?
   a. Abolitionists hoped to protect black gains by demanding black enfranchisement.
   b. Republicans wanted to prevent Southern political domination by the Democrats.
   c. Industrialists wanted to revive the system of plantation agriculture and profit from cheap cotton.

Fill-in-the-Blank

1. The _____ Amendment to the Constitution prohibited slavery in the United States.

2. The _____ were Southern state laws passed after the Civil War which severely restricted the civil and political rights of the former slaves.

3. The _____ was the federal protective and welfare agency established by Congress in March 1865 to aid and guide the former slaves in their transition from slavery to freedom.

4. The Southern _____ opened up public lands for resettlement by all settlers regardless of race, and each head of family received eighty acres from the government.

5. Frederick Douglass assumed the position of president of the _____ in 1874, but pressures born of political influence and the depression of 1873 caused its collapse.

True/False

1. Reconstruction is best understood as the period of African-
    American rule in the postwar South.

2. During Reconstruction black men held public office in the
    Southern states.

3. The Freedmen's Bureau was hindered in its task by Southern
    hostility and inefficiency among its own officials.

4. The largest number of African Americans elected to the U.S.
    House of Representatives was sent by South Carolina.

5. Lincoln viewed secession as an act of insurrection on the part of
    individuals within states: states had no authority to secede.

Relevance Today

1. Conflict between the executive and legislative branches of
    government during Reconstruction constituted one of the greatest
    power struggles in American history. What parallels exist between
    Andrew Johnson's struggle with and impeachment at the hands of
    Moderate and Radical Republicans and Bill Clinton's
    impeachment affair, 1998–1999?

2. Throughout history many of those with power have used a "divide
    and conquer" strategy toward those with less power. During
    Reconstruction, capitalists in America readily defeated white
    laborers in their contests for better wages and work conditions by
    using African Americans as strikebreakers. This, of course,
    engendered white labor hostility and prejudice toward blacks.
    What recent examples of this "divide and conquer" strategy can
    you find in business; higher education; or local, state, or national
    politics or within or among organizations you are connected to in

some way? Do you think that the benefits to the "divider" outweigh the negative and perhaps long-term consequences of such a policy?

3.   Franklin and Moss assert that, while the white leaders of the South were preoccupied with opposing black suffrage and civil rights, Northern financiers and industrialists took advantage of the opportunity to impose their economic control on the South. Historians and economists have demonstrated the folly of this policy: segregation and discrimination were enormously costly to the South both in terms of living standards and wasted human capital. Do you believe that your school, family, or friends expend time and energy wastefully preoccupied with concerns for social status and appearances? Do American leaders have the responsibility to promote the long-term economic interests of people? Should each citizen be responsible for securing his or her own best interests?

CHAPTER 13
LOSING THE PEACE

THEMES AND MAJOR POINTS

The struggle immediately after the Civil War between organized Southern whites on the one hand and the Union League, the Freedmen's Bureau, federal troops, and blacks on the other was essentially a struggle for political control of the South. The peace brought by the victory of the North could not prevail in such a warlike atmosphere.

Reconstruction came to a gradual end as restraints on the white South were relaxed and the stringent legislation designed to bring political and racial reform to the region was repealed. By 1876, whites in the South were once more able to rule the region without Northern interference or black influence.

After the Democrats came to power, efforts to disfranchise blacks moved toward success, slowed only briefly by the political revolt of white farmers in the 1890s. Once the farmers' revolt collapsed, however, Southern whites reunited to effect the complete disfranchisement of African-American voters.

With Southern blacks eliminated from the political arena, everything else necessary to ensure white supremacy was done. African Americans' economic opportunities were curtailed ruthlessly, and rigid segregation of the races was enforced by law and custom.

KEY EVENTS

1866   Knights of the Ku Klux Klan formed.

1871   Congress repealed the "iron-clad" oath provision of the
        Reconstruction Act.

1873   Panic of 1873 occurred.

1875   Civil Rights Act barring discrimination in public places and on
        public carriers enacted. Tennessee enacted the first "Jim Crow"
        law.

1876   Compromise of 1876: Reconstruction ended.

1883   Supreme Court overturned the Civil Rights Act of 1875.

1886   Colored Farmers' National Alliance and Cooperative Union
        formed.

1896   U.S. Supreme Court upholds segregation in *Plessy v. Ferguson*
        decision.

CHAPTER OVERVIEW

Congressional or "Radical" Reconstruction was hated from the
outset by most white Southerners. To them, Radical or "black"
Reconstruction subjected the South to the rule of blacks and "negro-loving
Yankees who encouraged African Americans in the belief that they were
equal to whites. Largely excluded from voting in the immediate aftermath
of the Civil War, these white Southerners observed their legislatures filled
with scalawags, carpetbaggers, and, much to their horror, African
Americans. Not surprisingly, Southern whites did little to cooperate with
the "radical" governments. In fact, numerous white supremacist and
paramilitary organizations formed in response to "Black Republicanism,"
and these groups precluded the creation of both stable economic
institutions and a harmonious society.

Southern social instability interfered considerably with the designs of Northern industrialists who were anxious to exploit the South's natural resources and to integrate the region into the Northern industrial economy. Once Northern businesses, which constituted an important base of Republican power, conceded Southern local rule as the price of economic integration, Reconstruction came to a close.

The Compromise of 1876, which ended the period of Reconstruction, was remarkably similar to the Compromises of 1820 and 1850, insofar as each came heavily at the expense of African Americans. Both before and after 1876, Southern blacks witnessed the elimination of the Republican Party in the South. As cotton prices plunged and the economic lot of Southern whites worsened, both racist demagoguery and the movement to consign blacks to an inferior position in society spread. After the collapse of the Populist revolt in 1896, the movement for complete disenfranchisement of blacks helped unite the white South. And from this unity emerged the system of Jim Crow or legalized segregation that pervaded the South into the 1960s. Sanctioned by the United States Supreme Court, codified racial segregation would serve as the cornerstone of the Southern political order emerging at the start of the twentieth century.

REVIEW QUESTIONS

Chapter Content Review

1.   What rhetoric were Republicans quick to use when speaking of their Democratic rivals?

2.   Why did Republicans seek to extend suffrage to the freedmen?

3.   What organizations formed during Johnsonian Reconstruction to intimidate both former slaves and Republican sympathizers alike? What was the goal of such groups as the Knights of the White Camelia and the Ku Klux Klan?

4.   Why was the struggle waged in the South from 1865 to 1877 essentially a political struggle?

5.   What steps did Congress take beginning in 1869 to restore Southern home rule?

6.   Describe the methods used by white Democrats to oust Radical rule in Louisiana, South Carolina, and Mississippi?

7.   Why was the Republican presidential victory in 1876 a victory for Southern Democrats?

8.   What tactics, other than intimidation and terror, did Southern Democrats use to restrict or control black suffrage?

9.   What economic forces undermined white unity in the 1880s and 1890s?

10.   How did the Populist challenge to Democratic power affect black voting in the South?

11.   What lessons did the Democrats and white Populists learn about black suffrage in the 1890s? In consequence, what did they agree to do?

12.   How did Mississippi disenfranchise blacks in 1890?

13.   What impact did the disenfranchisement laws have on Louisiana and Alabama at the start of the twentieth century?

14.   What was the cost to the South for maintaining a rigid white supremacist society?

Identification Questions

You should be able to describe the following key terms, concepts, individuals, and places and explain their significance:

1. Union League of America
2. Knights of the Ku Klux Klan
3. *United States v. Cruikshank*
4. Patrons of Husbandry
5. Colored Farmers' National Alliance and Cooperative Union
6. Tom Watson
7. Populist Party
8. poll tax
9. literacy test
10. "grandfather clause"
11. white primaries
12. *Plessy v. Ferguson,* 1896

ESSAY QUESTIONS

1. Discuss the reasons for the decline of Radical Reconstruction, 1869–1876.

2. While having virtually no political power in the South after 1896, Southern blacks were the major focus of all Southern state politic. Explain this paradox.

SELF-TEST

Multiple-Choice

1. To understand the politics of the Reconstruction period, the student should become familiar with
    a. the determination of the Republicans to strengthen their position and perpetuate their power.
    b. the pressure of industrialists for favorable legislation.
    c. conflicting philosophies of Reconstruction.
    d. all of the above.

2. In the movement to disenfranchise blacks completely through legal means, the South used as prerequisites to voting
    a. the "grandfather clause."
    b. payment of a poll tax.
    c. the ability to read or interpret the Constitution.
    d. all of the above.

3. Which one of the following did not support the Republican postwar goal of building a strong Southern wing of the party?
    a. the Freedmen's Bureau officials
    b. the Knights of the White Camelia
    c. the Union League of America
    d. missionary groups and teachers from the North

4. Which of the following organizations was not a radical agrarian organization?
    a. National Grange
    b. Southern Farmers Alliance
    c. Knights of Labor
    d. Colored Farmers' Alliance

5.   The white politician who said, "I am just as opposed to Booker
        Washington as a voter, with all his Anglo-Saxon re-enforcements,
        as I am to the coconut-headed, chocolate-colored, typical little
        coon, Andy Dotson, who blacks my boots every morning," was
        a.   J. K. Vardaman.
        b.   Ben Tillman.
        c.   James H. Young.
        d.   D.W. Boatner.

Fill-in-the-Blank

1.   _____. In the late nineteenth century, the Southern
        wing of _____, a political group/party of farmers,
        supported, for a brief time, the right of black men to vote.

2.   A protective and benevolent but, most important, political
        organization, _____ was the most active agency in the
        recruitment of blacks in the postwar South for the Republican
        Party.

3.   Two of the three states of the former Confederacy that remained
        under Republican control in 1876 were _____ and
        _____.

4.   In South Carolina, the disappointed and defeated white Populist
        politician _____ reversed an earlier opposite position
        and supported a constitutional amendment excluding blacks from
        the franchise.

5.   In Mississippi, the only black delegate to the state constitutional
        convention, _____ supported the amendment that
        disenfranchised the bulk of the state's black voters.

True/False

1. By 1876, the North had grown weary of the crusade for blacks in the South.

2. The movement for disenfranchisement of blacks was aided by the use of intimidation and violence.

3. One of the results of Radical Reconstruction was the eventual emergence of the "solid South."

4. Decisions of the United States Supreme Court had the effect of postponing the overthrow of Radical Reconstruction.

5. The leading religious denominations in the North called for a new Civil War to prevent the disenfranchisement of African Americans in the South.

Relevance Today

1. At the end of the Civil War, Southern whites sought to overthrow the political reforms imposed by the North and to dominate the black community. What rules and principles do you think should govern differences of opinion between citizens in a democracy such as the United States?

2. By 1876, whites in the South were once more able to rule the region without Northern interference or black influence. Can true democracy exist in places where one group of citizens has more power than any other? Do such situations exist in any part of the United States today?

3.   White Populists joined with other whites in disenfranchising blacks when they could not control the black vote in every election and on every issue. Is it fair for a powerful group of citizens to strip a less powerful group of its political rights because the weaker group does not behave as the powerful one thinks it should? Does this ever happen in the United States today?

4.   After 1876, the white South established a caste system based on white supremacy. Are there still signs of white supremacy in America today?

CHAPTER 14
PHILANTHROPY AND SELF-HELP

THEMES AND MAJOR TOPICS

Education, cherished by African Americans, was promoted and supported financially by black communities, churches, and philanthropic organizations.

Educational foundations and their contributors were motivated both by a desire to stimulate black efforts at self-help and by their sense of noblesse oblige.

Despite the largesse of philanthropists, they did little to encourage the equitable distribution of public funds for all Southern children; consequently, Southern whites grossly underfunded black public education, sometimes spending only one-tenth for black children what they spent for whites.

Booker T. Washington was the most important African-American leader in his day. Despite his many achievements and contribution to racial advancement, his advice often revealed a gap in his understanding of the changes wrought by industrial developments and their impact on black labor.

Rural existence grew increasingly bleak for African Americans, and they fled both their communities and states for opportunities in American cities both inside and outside the South.

Exclusion of African Americans from most political, economic, and social organizations in America induced them to establish independent self-help and support organizations to promote racial advancement.

Black churches continued to grow in number, and they continued to serve African-American economic, social, and political interests.

At the turn of the century, the voices of the "Talented-Tenth," America's black elite, began to be heard as a variety of black literary figures and newspapers proliferated.

KEY EVENTS

1867   Peabody Education Fund established.

1868   Freedmen's Bureau dissolved.

1881   Tuskeegee Institute founded.

1882   John F. Slater fund established.

1890   Afro-American League founded.

1897   American Negro Academy established.

1900   National Negro Business League established.

1903   General Education Board established.
        Souls of Black Folk published.

CHAPTER OVERVIEW

At the end of Reconstruction, Southern whites seemed more tolerant of educational institutions for blacks than of any of the other agencies African Americans established in order to improve themselves. The pursuit of education, therefore, came to be one of the greatest pre-occupations of blacks, and knowledge was viewed by many as the greatest single opportunity to escape the increasing proscriptions and indignities that whites were heaping on blacks.

Between 1880 and 1930, supporters of black education debated whether African Americans should receive limited education, or a special amount or kind of education, or have access to all the forms of education and training available to white Americans. Among African Americans, the most significant exchange regarding these options took place between Booker T. Washington and W.E.B. Du Bois.

Coincident with the growth of black schools in the South was the appearance of philanthropic educational foundations, funded heavily by wealthy white Americans. These agencies did much to broaden the concept of education for blacks in the South and to successfully stimulate self-help on the part of the individual, the institution, and the states of the South.

During a period of American history characterized by sharply declining economic, political, and social opportunities for nonwhites, African Americans were convinced that they had to rely chiefly on themselves. As a consequence, they expended enormous energy and creativity in their efforts to make a living and to meet the economic, educational, and social service needs of their race.

REVIEW QUESTIONS

Chapter Content Review

1.   What institution replaced the Freedmen's Bureau as the primary supporter of black schools in the South after Reconstruction?

2.   What educational aid foundations worked directly to advance the cause of black education in the United States.

3. How did the objectives of church-sponsored philanthropy differ from those of educational foundation philanthropy?

4. Did Northern philanthropists advocate the cause of black civil rights in the South?

5. In what ways did Southern blacks contribute to the growth and financial stability of their educational institutions?

6. By what means did Booker T. Washington believe blacks in the South would achieve success?

7. Why was Washington's emphasis on industrial or vocational education acceptable to both Southern whites and most people throughout the North?

8. Why was Washington himself regarded so highly by white leaders?

9. What criticism did W.E.B. Du Bois make regarding Booker T. Washington's emphasis on black vocational training and his de-emphasis of civil and political rights for blacks?

10. What criticisms does your textbook make of Washington's ideas?

11. What factors made it difficult for blacks to purchase farms after the Civil War?

12. By what means did white Southerners attempt to restrict the ability of Southern blacks to migrate north or west?

13. Why was life in the Southern urban centers both frustrating and unattractive to Southern blacks after Reconstruction?

14. To what degree did blacks succeed in participating in the life of national labor organizations? Explain.

15. Why did businesses both owned and operated by blacks emerge in large numbers throughout urban areas of America during the late nineteenth and early twentieth centuries?

16. What influence did better educated and more progressive black church members have over the direction of their religious communities?

17. In what ways did the black churches promote both education and social improvements?

Identification Questions

You should be able to describe the following key terms, concepts, individuals, and places and explain their significance:

1. Freedmen's Aid Society
2. George Peabody
3. John F. Slater
4. John D. Rockefeller
5. Anna T. Jeanes
6. Jubilee Singers
7. Booker T. Washington
8. Tuskeegee Institute
9. doctrine of industrial education
10. W.E.B. Du Bois
11. Jan E. Matzelinger
12. Elijah McCoy
13. Afro-American League
14. T. Thomas Fortune
15. American Negro Academy
16. *Up from Slavery* (1890)
17. *The Colored Cadet at West Point* (1889)
18. George Washington Williams

19. Charles Chesnutt
20. Paul Laurence Dunbar
21. Issac Murphy
22. Andrew "Rube" Foster

Essay Questions

1. Compare and contrast the philosophies of Booker T. Washington
    and W.E.B. Du Bois. To what extent was Du Bois's criticism of
    industrial education valid? To what extent was it invalid?

2. Black "self-help" took numerous forms after the Civil War.
    Explain why self-help, vis-à-vis governmental assistance, was
    necessary, and discuss several of the most successful and
    beneficial self-help efforts devised by African Americans at this
    time.

SELF-TEST

Multiple-Choice

1. Which of the following people provided substantial financial
    assistance for the education of Southern blacks?
    a. John F. Slater
    b. George Peabody
    c. Anna T. Jeanes
    d. all of the above

2. Booker T. Washington and W.E.B. Du Bois
   a. shared identical philosophies regarding the advancement of African Americans.
   b. expressed disinterest in political and civil rights for blacks.
   c. were in agreement as to the type of education blacks most needed.
   d. advocated programs of racial advancement.

3. One basic reason that large numbers of African Americans did not become a permanent part of the organized labor movement was
   a. that most were too lazy to work.
   b. that since the majority of black workers were skilled, they could make more money outside of the unions.
   c. that most white workers were prejudiced against black workers and sought to exclude them.
   d. that black laborers chose to remain aloof.

4. A factor that made it difficult for African Americans to become successful farmers was
   a. a lack of knowledge about marketing crops and purchasing supplies.
   b. a lack of knowledge about modern agricultural methods.
   c. white reluctance to sell land to African Americans.
   d. all of the above.

5. Which of the following men distinguished himself as the three-time winner of the Kentucky Derby and as the victor in 44 percent of the races he competed in during his lifetime?
   a. Charles Chesnutt
   b. Andrew Rube Foster
   c. Jack Johnson
   d. Issac Murphy

Fill-in-the-Blank

1. _____ opposed the exodus of blacks from the South on the grounds that the government should protect citizens wherever they lived.

2. _____, which placed little emphasis on skills, was the only labor union that made black workers welcome as members.

3. _____ was the author of *The Suppression of the African Slave Trade,* the first scientific historical monograph written by a black man.

4. _____ patented fifty inventions relating principally to automatic lubricators for machines.

5. Founded in 1897, the _____ promoted the exchange of ideas among black intellectuals and helped perpetuate the black protest tradition in an age of accommodation and proscription.

True/False

1. Philanthropists contributed substantially to the improvement of education for African Americans in the South.

2. Philanthropists did much to encourage the equitable distribution of tax money for educating Southern youth.

3. The doctrine of vocational education for the black masses met with the general disapproval of most whites.

4.   All black leaders agreed that it was desirable for blacks to leave the South and seek work elsewhere.

5.   Rural blacks found that the cities to which they fled offered abundant opportunities to enjoy economic benefits and political gains.

Relevance Today

1.   Debates regarding the types and extent of education for blacks swirled in the late nineteenth and early twentieth centuries. Booker T. Washington advocated industrial education, or education that could provide training for skills that jwould provide economic gain for blacks and their communities. W.E.B. Du Bois objected to Washington's almost exclusive emphasis on economic advancement. He advocated a liberal arts curriculum and felt that schools should develop "intelligence, broad sympathy, knowledge of the world as it is, and of the relation of men to it." Similar debates swirl today with respect to both public and higher education. Who should make the decision to determine the type of education our society offers its children? Do you feel that offering training in practical skills meets the needs of most people? Should schools remove liberal arts curricula that have no immediately discernible value?

2.   B.T. Washington's conciliatory approach to whites in the "Age of Washington" led many black leaders after 1960 to view him, in retrospect, as "an Uncle Tom." What circumstances do you feel necessitate that individual leaders act in a conciliatory manner?

3.   At the inaugural meeting of the American Negro Academy in 1897, it was proposed that several women be admitted to membership. The proposal was rejected based on the argument that women would render the group a social rather than a learned society. When asked by a reporter what position women were to assume in SNCC (Student Non-violent Coordinating Committee), Stokely Carmichael replied, "Supine." To what extent do you believe sexism damages the credibility of any civil rights organization? Do you believe that moral leadership, in order to transform society, must rid itself of all racial, ethnic, and other forms of prejudice?

CHAPTER 15
THE COLOR LINE

THEMES AND MAJOR POINTS

During the late nineteenth and early twentieth centuries, the United States became an international imperialist power with newly acquired colonies in the West Indies, the Pacific Islands, Asia, and Central America. African Americans were involved in the military actions that brought these territories under the control of the United States.

The United States' new colonial empire was constituted almost wholly of territories where the chief economic activity was agriculture and whose populations were overwhelmingly nonwhite. Subjection to U.S. rule meant that the racial policies of the South, including white supremacy and segregation, became normative in these territories.

As American cities grew in numbers and importance, separate black communities appeared or expanded within them, most with numerous visible economic, political, and social problems.

North and south, the pattern of violence against African Americans escalated.

The steadily expanding mistreatment, violence, and discrimination faced by blacks moved a group of young African Americans to establish a race defense organization known as the Niagara Movement. Eventually, the members of the Niagara Movement joined with a group of white reformers to establish the National Association for the Advancement of Colored People.

KEY EVENTS

1867   United States purchased Alaska.

1898   Spanish-American War began.
        Hawaii was annexed.

1899   American occupation of the Philippines began.

1903   America acquired the Panama Canal zone.

1905   Niagara Movement began.

1906   Brownsville, Texas, riot occurred.

1908   Springfield, Illinois, riot occurred.

1909   NAACP formed.

1911   National Urban League formed.

1916   United States landed marines in Santa Domingo.

1917   United States placed Haiti under military rule.
        America purchased the Virgin Islands from Denmark.

CHAPTER OVERVIEW

For the United States, two of the most far-reaching consequences of Reconstruction and the economic revolution that accomplished it were the end of national isolation and the pursuit of imperialism. America's victory in the Spanish-American War was the major event that transformed the United States into a full-fledged imperial power. It was ironic that African-American soldiers, themselves subject to racist restrictions and viewed as inferiors by most white Americans, should have played a part in bringing extensive numbers of other nonwhites under the domination of the United States. Unlike other imperial powers, however, the United States had a "color problem" at home and, therefore, had to pursue in its colonies a policy with regard to race that would not upset its segregationist racial policy at home.

Coincident with the rise of the city in American life was the appearance of the African-American ghetto within the city. Though drawn to the cities just as other Americans were for increased economic opportunities, blacks experienced residential segregation, difficulty in securing anything except the most onerous and least attractive jobs, and violent attacks from whites, who viewed them as invaders of their living and employment spaces. The most strenuous efforts to address these problems came from the National Association for the Advancement of Colored People (NAACP) and the National Urban League.

REVIEW QUESTIONS

Chapter Content Review

1.   What factors contributed to the United States' growing interest in world affairs after the Civil War?

2.   When America declared war on Spain in 1898, most black Americans were anxious to assist their nation in liberating the Cuban people. What views were expressed by the anti-imperialist blacks of America?

3.   What two wars did the black troops of America face in 1898?

4.   To what extent were the famed "roughriders" under Teddy Roosevelt indebted to the Ninth and Tenth (Colored) Cavalry units?

5. What racial considerations made the U.S. Congress reluctant to grant full political rights to Caribbean and Latin American peoples at the turn of the century?

6. Explain the means by which the United States forced Haiti and Santa Domingo into its sphere.

7. In which African nation did the United States extend its "dollar diplomacy" in the first quarter of the twentieth century?

8. What did President Roosevelt's dinner with Booker T. Washington signify to Southern whites? What did President Roosevelt's dinner with Booker T. Washington signify to African Americans?

9. What difficulties arose when blacks in the early 1900s migrated to cities?

10. One "muckraker" from the ranks of the progressives, Ray Stannard Baker, discussed the "Negro problem" in his book, *Following the Color Line*. What was his solution to the "problem"?

11. How did Teddy Roosevelt's action taken in response to the Brownsville, Texas, incident of 1906 ultimately discredit him in the eyes of African Americans?

12. Why were the race riots at the start of the twentieth century so disillusioning and threatening to American blacks? In what way did they refute Booker T. Washington's theories?

13. In what way did W.E.B. Du Bois, John Dewey, Jane Addams, and other progressives respond to these riots?

Identification Questions

You should be able to describe the following key terms, concepts, individuals, and places and explain their significance:

1. Quintin Bandara
2. Colonel James H. Young
3. Emilio Aguinaldo
4. William Hastie
5. William D. Crum
6. Niagara Movement
7. NAACP
8. *Crisis*
9. National Urban League
10. *Guinn v. United States* (1915)
11. *Buchanan v. Warley* (1917)
12. *Moore v. Dempsey* (1923)

Essay Questions

1. While American imperialism adversely affected a multitude of nonwhite peoples around the world, African Americans played a substantial role in American imperialist ventures. Explain.

2. Explain why "self-help" and private philanthropy were at best only partial solutions to the problems confronting American blacks at the beginning of the twentieth century.

SELF-TEST

Multiple-Choice

1. The term applied to the black soldiers by Spaniards in the Spanish-American War was
    a. Black Thunderbolts.
    b. Smoked Yankees.
    c. Muckrakers.
    d. Butchers.

2. United States imperialism included annexing all of the following except
    a. Hawaii.
    b. Formosa.
    c. the Philippines.
    d. Puerto Rico.

3. As president, Theodore Roosevelt pleased African Americans when he
    a. dined with Booker T. Washington.
    b. appointed a black man to the collectorship of the port of Charleston.
    c. refused to accept the forced resignation of the black postmistress at Indianola, Mississippi.
    d. all of the above.

4. What territory did the United States add to its colonial empire in 1917?
    a. the Virgin Islands
    b. Bermuda
    c. Cancun
    d. Samoa

5. In May 1916, United States marines occupied the oldest republic in North and South America, the country of
   a. Mexico.
   b. Panama.
   c. Haiti.
   d. Cuba.

Fill-in-the-Blank

1. West Pointer _____ was the only black commissioned officer in the country at the outbreak of the Spanish-American War.

2. _____ was the leader of the Niagara Movement and the first editor of *Crisis,* published by the NAACP.

3. The _____ successfully widened opportunites for blacks in finding industrial employment and in helping black people to solve problems peculiar to the cities.

4. The country in West Africa that was in all essentials a protectorate of the United States was _____.

5. Though _____, the African-American postmistress of Indianola, Mississippi, was pressured by white citizens to resign; President Theodore Roosevelt refused to accept her resignation.

True/False

1. During the first quarter of the twentieth century, some municipalities gave official sanction to the practice of residential segregation.

2. Coincident with the rise of the American city was the rise of the black community within the city.

3. It was in Africa that the United States pursued its new imperialistic policy most vigorously.

4. At the outbreak of the Spanish-American War, there were no African-American units in the regular army.

5. The August 1908 race riots in Springfield, Illinois, shocked many whites and moved some to do something to help African Americans.

Relevance Today

1. Many African Americans were eager and active participants in the military actions that gave the United States an overseas colonial empire. How do you think African Americans today feel about the relationship of the United States to weaker, nonwhite countries?

2. In the late nineteenth and early twentieth centuries, separate, predominantly black residential sections appeared or expanded in U.S. cities. Are the separate, predominantly black residential sections in U.S. cities and suburbs shrinking or expanding today? How do you account for the change?

3. As the twentieth century began, throughout the United States the pattern of violence against African Americans escalated. There is a pattern of violence against African Americans in the United States today. Do all American citizens have a responsibility to work to stop violence against African Americans and other American citizens who are victims of violence? Why or why not?

CHAPTER 16
IN PURSUIT OF DEMOCRACY

THEMES AND MAJOR TOPICS

Despite his promises of "seeing justice done to the colored people in every matter," President Woodrow Wilson segregated African-American federal employees by executive order and phased out most of them from federal civil service.

As a rule, African Americans eagerly sought to participate in the nation's war effort.

The rampant discrimination suffered by blacks—in the armed services, in war industries, and in their communities—steadily decreased black enthusiasm for World War I.

W.E.B. Du Bois called a Pan-African Congress in 1918 to focus attention on the issues facing people of color in various parts of the world.

World War I accelerated the pace of black migration from the South; opportunities for higher pay and the promise of greater freedom fueled this process.

The talk of democracy surrounding America's involvement in the First World War raised the hopes of African Americans that the war's end would usher in a new period of opportunity for them, both in the area of economic life and in the sphere of civil rights.

KEY EVENTS

1912   Woodrow Wilson elected president.

1913   Wilson issued an executive order requiring the segregation of
        black federal workers.

1914   World War I began.

1915   Booker T. Washington died.

1917   United States declared war on the Central Powers.

1918   World War I ended.

CHAPTER OVERVIEW

Although African Americans felt extremely discouraged by the increase in segregation during the first years of Woodrow Wilson's presidency, the entrance of the United States into World War I stimulated them to express their patriotism by volunteering for military service in large numbers, through support of wartime emergency measures, and by generous purchase of war bonds. Most hoped that these expressions of devotion to their country would strengthen the claims of minorities to equal rights and undermine segregation. While sizable numbers of African Americans served in the U.S. army at home and abroad, segregation remained intact, and numerous blacks wearing the uniform of their country were objects of hostility and violence from whites.

American domestic mobilization for the First World War had profound consequences for the African-American community. The expansion of American industries, coupled with the shortage of white native and immigrant laborers, created numerous employment opportunities for African Americans. These opportunities intensified the migration of Southern blacks to Northern urban centers, causing thousands of African Americans to enter America's cities in search of greater economic, political, and social freedom. These burgeoning black communities increasingly came into conflict with surrounding and unwelcoming white neighbors.

REVIEW QUESTIONS

Chapter Content Review

1. Why did African Americans reject the candidacy of Teddy Roosevelt and his Bull Moose Party in the election of 1912?

2. Why did much of the legislation proposed in Congress in 1915 dismay black Americans?

3. How did the U.S. Congress and the nation's military recruitment offices respond to attempts by blacks to serve their nation either as common soldiers or officers?

4. Why was the process of training black regiments so problematic for the War Department?

5. What was the War Department's solution to the problem encountered when the townsfolk of Spartanburg, South Carolina, precipitated a controversy with the black Fifteenth New York Infantry?

6. What contributions did black stevedores make in the war effort?

7. Were the African-American regiments who fought with the French in 1918 major contributors in the war effort? Explain.

8. What tactics did the German army use in attempting to weaken the efforts of African Americans to subdue them? Did they succeed?

9. How were the African-American troops treated by the French citizens?

10. In what ways did African Americans express their commitment to the war effort?

11. What forces induced hundreds of thousands of blacks to migrate from the South during the War?

12. Why would white Southerners create numerous obstacles to black migration?

13. What role did the National Urban League play in the process of black migration?

Identification Questions

You should be able to describe the following key terms, concepts, individuals, and places and explain their significance:

1. *Birth of a Nation*
2. Emmett J. Scott
3. stevedore regiments
4. 369th United States Infantry
5. Henry Johnson
6. Pan-African Congress (1919)
7. *Secret Information Concerning Black Troops*
8. A. Philip Randolph
9. Chandler Owen
10. *The Messenger*

Essay Questions

1. Discuss the various types of discrimination practiced against American blacks both immediately prior to and during World War I, and explain why African Americans would, despite their mistreatment, enlist in the military and support the war effort so fervently.

2. Ironically, at the same time that Americans fought to "make the world safe for democracy," democracy was being undermined in the United States. Explain.

SELF-TEST

Multiple-Choice

1. By executive order, President Woodrow Wilson
   a. segregated black federal employees in eating and rest room facilities.
   b. phased out most blacks from the civil service.
   c. did both a and b.
   d. did neither a nor b.

2. The movie *Birth of a Nation*
   a. glorified black manhood.
   b. told a positive and accurate story of black emancipation.
   c. was blatantly antiblack.
   d. received little, if any, attention from the public.

3. During World War I, blacks were barred entirely from the
   a. cavalry.
   b. marines.
   c. engineer corps.
   d. stevedores.

4.	During the First World War,
	a.	black Americans stopped being victims of lynching and other forms of violence in America.
	b.	all African-American publications condemned U.S. participation in the war.
	c.	hundreds of black men served as officers in the U.S. army.
	d.	the Germans resorted to propaganda to sway African-American sympathies.

5.	The highest-ranking black officer in the U.S. army on the eve of World War I was
	a.	Emmett J. Scott.
	b.	Henry Johnson.
	c.	Chandler Owen.
	d.	Charles Young.

Fill-in-the-Blank

1.	The black U.S. infantry regiment _____ was called "hell fighters" by the Germans and for their bravery won the French Croix de Guerre.

2.	The black newspaper _____ published in New York by A. Philip Randolph and Chandler Owen, refused to support the war effort as almost all other black publications did.

3.	_____ was appointed special assistant to the Secretary of War and served him as confidential advisor on matters relating to the African Americans.

4.	_____ is the sensational feat of a black private in helping to repulse a German raiding party in May 1918.

5.   The nation of _____ dismayed many white Americans during and after the First World War by treating African-American soldiers with respect and dignity.

True/False

1.   There was a surprising lack of friction between American white Southerners and African-American soldiers during the war.

2.   The first black servicemen to arrive in Europe were combat troops.

3.   The black press, for the most part, supported the war with enthusiasm.

4.   Large numbers of African Americans migrated out of the South westward and northward toward war industries in urban centers.

5.   Southern business and political leaders encouraged black migration.

Relevance Today

1.   U.S. racial policies during World War I revealed many inefficiencies born of prejudice. Separate white and black barracks, separate training facilities, and other segregated institutions both increased costs and reduced the nation's ability to prosecute the war effectively. What types of services and facilities are segregated (racially or otherwise) today, and are these practices economical? What drives the decision for separation in these circumstances?

2.   Despite the enormous benefits that Southern blacks could secure in Northern cities, most chose to remain in the South (see table 6 of chapter 16). What factors do you think influenced many Southern blacks to remain in the South? Do you think that the incredible mobility of Americans in the 1990s has had an adverse affect on society? Why or why not?

CHAPTER 17
DEMOCRACY ESCAPES

THEMES AND MAJOR POINTS

After World War I, blacks found that their patriotic support of the United States, on the battlefield and the home front, had done little to expand freedom and democracy for them. Indeed, their situation worsened as the Ku Klux Klan expanded its terrorism against blacks and the nation was rocked with race riots that took a high toll of black lives. In this postwar strife, African Americans fought and died in self-defense with a fierceness that proclaimed their determination to save democracy in the United States of America.

Black organizations repeatedly protested the failure of the United States to grant African Americans first-class citizenship, with the National Association for the Advancement of Colored People taking the lead in the call for a federal law against lynching. The great support received by Marcus Garvey and his Universal Negro Improvement Association was a public endorsement by African Americans of Garvey's concept of black pride and a statement of their contempt for the moral and political hypocrisy of racist white Americans.

KEY EVENTS

1916   Knights of the Ku Klux Klan grew to more than 100,000.

1918–1919   African-American servicemen return to U.S. after World War I.

1918   Race riots broke out and other expressions of racial strife occurred.

The NAACP began effort to secure passage of a federal antilynching law.

George Baker, known as "Father Divine," found an interracial religious community that addressed the practical and spiritual needs of some African Americans.

1916–1920	Marcus Garvey established the Universal Negro Improvement Association (UNIA) as part of the first mass movement among African Americans.
1919	The Commission on Interracial Cooperation established.
1923	U.S. Congress failed to pass a federal anti-lynching bill.
1925	Marcus Garvey entered a United States federal prison to begin serving a five-year sentence for mail fraud.
1927	Marcus Garvey pardoned and deported by President Calvin Coolidge.

CHAPTER OVERVIEW

Black American veterans of World War I were welcomed home enthusiastically by their communities. They were also confronted by the Ku Klux Klan, whose resurgence reflected powerful sentiments among white Americans for the preservation of white supremacy and a deep resentment at the expanded black presence in America's cities and in jobs previously "for whites only." These tensions resulted in race riots that produced numerous black and white injuries and deaths, as well as considerable destruction of property.

In the African-American community, there were several responses to these conditions: the NAACP increased both its demands for black equality and its efforts to secure passage of a federal antilynching law in the United States Congress; Marcus Garvey and his black nationalist movement received widespread support from the black masses; and various black religious communities that promoted separatism and self-help grew in influence and numbers.

REVIEW QUESTIONS

Chapter Content Review

1. How did African-American soldiers who served abroad in World War I feel at the end of the war about returning to the United States?

2. What is the Ku Klux Klan? What are its major beliefs and goals?

3. What is a lynching? By whom were African Americans lynched in the aftermath of World War I? Why?

4. Why did James Weldon Johnson, the executive secretary of the NAACP, call the summer of 1919 "the red summer"?

5. What were the causes and consequences of the race riot in Chicago in July 1919? Why was it considered the most serious race riot that year?

6. In what way was the willingness of African-American riot victims to retaliate in their own defense a new factor in American race relations? What were the causes of this new behavior on the part of blacks? Why did some white Americans believe that "foreign influences" were responsible for African Americans' new assertiveness?

7. Who was Claude McKay? How did he contribute to greater understanding of new attitudes among African Americans?

8. What steps did the NAACP take to seek protection for African Americans in the aftermath of World War I? Were the efforts of the NAACP successful?

9. Who were the founders of the Commission on Interracial Cooperation (CIC)? What kind of work did it begin following World War I? How successful was the CIC?

10. Who was Marcus Garvey? Why did his organization grow so rapidly in the United States? What were the major beliefs and goals of the Garvey movement?

11. Was Garvey's movement a success or failure? Why?

12. Who was Father Divine? What kind of message and programs did he offer the African-American masses?

13. Were the message and programs of Father Divine helpful or harmful to American blacks? Explain.

Identification Questions

You should be able to describe the following key terms, concepts, individuals, and places and explain their significance:

1. Ninety-Second Division
2. Peace Mission
3. Dr. O. H. Sweet
4. Representative L. C. Dyer
5. Black Star Line
6. *Thirty Years of Lynching in the United States, 1889–1918*

Essay Questions

1. Why did white Americans fight in World War I to make the world "safe for democracy" and, at the conclusion of the war, refuse to grant equal rights to its African-American citizens?

2. Why do you think so many African Americans believed the ideas and programs of Marcus Garvey were the answer to their problems? Were Garvey's ideas correct and his solutions to problems practical?

3. Compare the post–World War I activities of the NAACP to promote the well-being of African Americans with the efforts of the UNIA to do the same thing. Which of the two organizations was more effective? Why?

SELF-TEST

Multiple-Choice

1. Which of the following most accurately describes the Ku Klux Klan of the postwar years?
    a. Unlike the first Klan, it welcomed black members.
    b. It was a racist, reactionary, white supremacist organization.
    c. Its membership was confined to the South.
    d. It condemned violence as a means of achieving its objectives.

2. An epidemic of race riots beginning in the summer of which of the following years led to its designation as the "Red Summer"?
    a. 1919
    b. 1920
    c. 1929
    d. 1930

3.	In *Smith v. Allwright,* the United States Supreme Court held that
	a.	the grandfather clause violated the Constitution.
	b.	residential segregation ordinances were unconstitutional.
	c.	each state must provide integrated educational opportunities for all citizens.
	d.	the exclusion of blacks from the Democratic primary was a violation of the Fifteenth Amendment.

4.	When African-American troops who had fought in World War I disembarked in New York City, their first reception was
	a.	enthusiastic.
	b.	hostile.
	c.	indifferent.

5.	The black poet whose poem began with the words "If we must die, let it not be like hogs" was
	a.	Langston Hughes.
	b.	Zora Neale Hurston.
	c.	W. E. B. Du Bois.
	d.	Claude McKay.

Fill-in-the-Blank

1.	_____ was the term applied to the summer of 1919 because of the intensity and widespread nature of racial strife then.

2.	_____ was the name of the black nationalist organization founded by the "Black Moses."

3.	The most successful black union of the postwar period, founded by A. Philip Randolph, was _____.

4.   _____ was the racist, reactionary white supremacist organization that was revived in 1915 and flourished in the United States in the 1920s.

5.   In 1923, the predominantly black town of _____, Florida, was annihilated by a white mob.

True/False

1.   Most black soldiers who served in France refused to return to the United States after the war.

2.   Hindering the work of the NAACP was its policy of excluding whites from membership.

3.   In the first signs of recession in the mid-1920s, large numbers of blacks lost their jobs.

4.   In 1921, the city of Tulsa, Oklahoma, celebrated a half-century of racial harmony.

5.   The Ku Klux Klan displayed a banner out of the windows of its New York office solemnly announcing "A man was lynched yesterday."

Relevance Today

1.   Following World War I, racist organizations such as the Ku Klux Klan grew in numbers and influence. Are racist organizations disappearing or growing in the United States today? Why?

2.   As blacks faced a barrage of racist attitudes and actions in the immediate aftermath of World War I and the decade of the 1920s, they increased their demands for better treatment and affirmed the idea of creating a separate black community that would not be dependent on whites for resources or respect. How do present-day groups in the African-American community respond to racist attitudes and actions? Does their response serve or disserve their interests?

CHAPTER 18
THE HARLEM RENAISSANCE

THEMES AND MAJOR POINTS

During the post–World War I period a distinct new literary movement—characterized by realism and social consciousness—emerged in the United States and gave impetus to the Harlem Renaissance.

Increasing racial confidence, coupled with impatience and bitterness born of the gap between the promises of freedom and the reality of their experiences, stimulated much of the creativity and articulation identified with the Harlem Renaissance.

The works and lives of the creative men and women who participated in the Harlem Renaissance reflect their search for answers to two significant questions: Is a black artist's highest responsibility to the work of art or to the progress of race? Can the two be reconciled?

Music, theatre, filmmaking, painting, sculpting, and other nonliterary forms of expression highlighted the tremendous diversity and wealth of African-American expression that came to fruition in the Harlem Renaissance.

KEY EVENTS

1920 Charles Gilpin starred in title role of *Emperor Jones*.

1921 *Shuffle Along* opened.
Claude McKay's *Harlem Shadows* published.

1923 Jean Toomer's *Cane* is released.
Liza, *Running Wild*, and *Chocolate Dandies* opened.

1924   Jessie Redmond Fauset's *There Is Confusion* is published.
        Paul Robeson performed in *All God's Chillun Got Wings.*

1925   Countee Cullen's first volume of poetry published as *Color.*
        Alain Locke edited the "Harlem Number," of *Survey Graphic.*

1926   Langston Hughes released *Weary Blues.*

1927   *Porgy* opened.

1928   Nella Larsen's *Quicksand* published.

1929   Jessie Redmond Fauset's *Plum Bun* released.

1932   Sterling Brown's *Southern Road* appeared.

1934   Zora Neale Hurston published *Jonah's Gourd Vine.*

1937   Zora Neale Hurston's *Their Eyes Were Watching God* published.

CHAPTER OVERVIEW

Following World War I, the work of leading white American intellectuals and artists reflected a shift toward realism and social consciousness. This stimulated the interest of African Americans in the arts and helped to create a receptive climate for the work of creative blacks in some influential and affluent segments of the white community. The outpouring of African-American artistic activity in the 1920s and 1930s, centered in (but not exclusive to) New York City's Harlem, was described at various times as the "Harlem Renaissance," the "Black Renaissance," or the "New Negro Movement."

The unifying theme in the varied creative activity of black novelists, short story writers, poets, painters, sculptors, filmmakers, dancers, singers, actors, art critics, and other contributors was their use of their talents to confront the racism and unfairness that shaped the black experience in an America controlled by whites.

REVIEW QUESTIONS

Chapter Content Review

1. Why did a number of white writers become interested in the American race problem following World War I?

2. Name three of these white writers and list the works they produced that reflected this interest.

3. What were the two important developments in the African-American community during and immediately after World War I that fostered the growth of the New Negro Movement?

4. What African-American community became most closely identified with the New Negro Movement? In what city was it located? Why did it come to be so closely associated with the movement?

5. List five of the major literary contributors to the Black Renaissance, including at least two women, and indicate their most important works.

6. Who were some of the actors and performers who expressed the spirit of the Black Renaissance in plays and musicals?

7. List the names and major works of several painters or sculptors who were a part of the New Negro Movement of the 1920s and 1930s.

8.   What African-American communities in southern and midwestern cities became significant centers of the Black Renaissance?

9.   Who were the people Zora Neale Hurston described as "Negrotarians"? What did she mean by this term?

10. Were all the African-American writers associated with the New Negro Movement "crusaders"? If some were not, what was their artistic motivation?

11. Who was probably the most prolific of the writers who contributed to the Black Renaissance?

12. What were the titles and who were the stars of some of the best-known and most popular black musical revues during the 1920s?

13. Describe the independent black film movement of the 1920s. Indicate the ways in which the New Negro Movement influenced the black independent film movement.

14. Name three jazz artists who were part of the Harlem Renaissance and list their contributions.

Identification Questions

You should be able to describe the following key terms, concepts, individuals, and places and explain their significance:

1.   Moorfield Story, *Problems of Today*
2.   "Yet Do I marvel at this curious thing/To Make a poet black, and bid him sing"
3.   *The Green Pastures*
4.   F. E. Miller, Aubrey Lyle, Eubie Blake, and Noble Sissle
5.   Florence Mills
6.   Roland Hayes

7. *The Banjo Lesson*
8. Zora Neale Hurston

Essay Questions

1. Discuss the ways in which white Americans' growing interest in social issues during the post-World War I period set the stage for the Black Renaissance.

2. Analyze how and why the African-American community in New York City became the most important cultural center in black America.

3. Were black women as much participants in the New Negro Movement as black males? If so, why do you think this was so? If not, why not?

SELF-TEST

Multiple-Choice

1. The Harlem Renaissance produced a talented assemblage of black
   a. professional basketball players.
   b. New York politicians.
   c. business leaders.
   d. writers.

2. Which of the following was responsible for producing the black writers who contributed to the Harlem Renaissance?
   a. the desire to stimulate the use of black English
   b. an attempt to produce literary works for an all-black audience
   c. a keener realization of injustice and the improvement of the capacity for expression

d.   the desire to embrace and publicize the doctrines of socialists and communists

3.   Marcus Garvey energized the New Negro Movement by
   a.   raising the consciousness of African Americans.
   b.   outraging many African-American leaders.
   c.   creating excitement for black and white Americans alike.
   d.   all of the above.

4.   All of the following groups associated with the Harlem Renaissance achieved some financial success for their work except
   a.   novelists.
   b.   musicians.
   c.   filmmakers.
   d.   painters.

5.   All of the following communities became significant centers of the Black Renaissance except
   a.   Washington, DC.
   b.   Nashville, TN.
   c.   Chicago, IL.
   d.   Birmingham, AL.

6.   The following represent several of the most significant writers of the Harlem Renaissance, with the exception of
   a.   Claude McKay.
   b.   Ferdinand Morton.
   c.   James Weldon Johnson.
   d.   Jean Toomer.

Fill-in-the-Blank

1.   *Crisis* and _____ were two of the first black publications to open their pages to African-American poets.

2. _____ was a brilliant black musical revue that opened in New York City in the summer of 1921.

3. Many students of the period contend that the Harlem Renaissance ended with the production of _____, which appeared in 1930.

4. _____, the leading graphic artist of the Harlem Renaissance, depicted the history of African Americans in his murals.

5. _____ was the most prolific writer of the Harlem Renaissance. Examples of his work include "The Negro Speaks of Rivers" and *Not Without Laughter*.

6. _____ was a poet, an essayist, and a novelist (*There Is Confusion*) whose characters reflect the growing Americanization of blacks.

True/False

1. The literature of the Harlem Renaissance was, for the most part, remarkably free of race consciousness.

2. Even before the 1920s, New York City had become the intellectual and cultural center of black America.

3. Before the 1920s came to an end, the creative forces of the Harlem Renaissance made themselves felt throughout the entire African-American community in the United States.

4. Awareness of the gap between the American promise of freedom and their own experiences made many African Americans bitter and defiant.

Relevance Today

1. The "New Negro Movement" or "Harlem Renaissance" first emerged in New York City. The Civil Rights Movement of the 1950s and 1960s coalesced primarily within the black churches scattered in Southern urban centers. The Nation of Islam has traditionally recruited large numbers of members from inside American prisons. What forces or factors related to location or place facilitate the emergence of significant political, social, or cultural movements? Are there factors or forces common to all of the above-mentioned groups/movements?

2. Many works that emerged from the Harlem Renaissance depict one of the most important themes of African-American history—the dual identity of black Americans. On the one hand, African Americans are Americans and have contributed handsomely to the country's multifaceted economic and cultural richness. They identify with notions of freedom and valor in defense of liberty. On the other hand, the distinctness of the African-American experience, including memories of slavery, racism, and rejection, has contributed to the formation of a unique African-American identity. What are some events that occur in the lives of African Americans today that serve as a reminder of the dual identity/dual existence of black Americans?

CHAPTER 19
THE NEW DEAL

THEMES AND MAJOR POINTS

During the Great Depression, millions of African Americans lost their jobs and were forced onto relief at rates higher than white Americans. Even at this time of crisis, blacks faced discriminations, for in few places was relief administered on a nonracial basis.

With the presidential election of 1936, African Americans began a steady movement toward the Democratic Party, attracted both by the New Deal policies of Franklin D. Roosevelt and the friendliness of his wife Eleanor Roosevelt to blacks. While the appeal of the Democratic Party to black Americans grew during the years Roosevelt was president, after 1940 the black vote was often divided between the Democrats and Republicans.

One of the most important factors that made black involvement in American political life once more acceptable to white Americans was President Franklin D. Roosevelt's policy of appointing African-American specialists and advisors in various federal government departments.

While African Americans benefited from the Roosevelt administration's New Deal agencies, there was discrimination against blacks in the way these agencies administered federal programs. Some impatient blacks used what force they could command to secure employment and relief.

During the Great Depression, the white labor movement, after decades of excluding the bulk of black workers and blatantly discriminating against the small number of blacks in its ranks, began a slow process of drawing African Americans into unions. This was one of the most significant developments in blacks' struggle for greater integration into American life.

KEY EVENTS

1925	Brotherhood of Sleeping Car Porters and Maids established.
1928	Oscar DePriest of Chicago, a black Republican, elected to the U.S. House of Representatives.
1929	Stock market crashed; "Great Depression" began.
1930	Nomination of John J. Parker to U.S. Supreme Court received strong opposition from the African-American community; Parker failed to win Senate approval.
1931	The "Jobs for Negroes" movement began in St. Louis.
1932	Angelo Herndon, a black member of the Communist Party, was arrested, tried, convicted, and sentenced to eighteen years in prison on the charge of inciting to insurrection. The nine "Scottsboro boys" were arrested on charges of rape.
1933	The Citizens League for Fair Play organized in New York City.
1934	Arthur W. Mitchell of Chicago, a black Democrat, defeated Oscar DePriest for re-election.
1935	African Americans rioted in New York City.
1935–1936	John L. Lewis established the Congress of Industrial Organizations (CIO).

1936   Majority of African Americans deserted the Republicans and voted Democratic in presidential election.

CHAPTER OVERVIEW

The desperate need of American blacks for economic relief during the Great Depression was expressed in self-help campaigns such as the "Jobs for Negroes" movement and the Citizens League for Fair Play. During the 1920s and increasingly in the 1930s, blacks began to involve themselves with the organized labor movement, despite widespread discrimination in most unions.

During the same years, more African Americans voted in local and national elections, making possible an increase in the number of black elected officials, including the election of the first black members of Congress since the end of Reconstruction. The New Deal programs of Franklin D. Roosevelt, however, and the activities of Eleanor Roosevelt and other liberal white New Dealers caused the majority of African Americans to shift from the Republican to the Democratic Party.

REVIEW QUESTIONS

Chapter Content Review

1.   What new areas of employment did African Americans enter in the decade following World War I?

2.   What was the most significant step in the 1920s toward the unionization of African Americans?

3.   What were the most important types of businesses in the African-American community in the two decades after World War I?

4. Did the situation of black American farmers improve or worsen from 1920 to 1940?

5. Once the Great Depression began, how were African Americans treated in the administration of relief services?

6. What were causes of the political resurgence in the African-American community from 1920 to 1940?

7. Why did many black voters begin to desert the Republican Party during the 1920s?

8. What was the name and party of the African American elected to the United States House of Representatives in 1928? What made it possible for him to win election?

9. Were African Americans strong supporters of the bid of Franklin D. Roosevelt for the U.S. presidency in 1932?

10. Was the Communist Party attractive to African Americans?

11. How did African Americans view Eleanor Roosevelt? Why?

12. What was the name and party of the African American elected to the United States House of Representatives in 1934? What made it possible for him to win election?

13. What was President Franklin D. Roosevelt's "Black Cabinet"? Who were some of its members? What were their responsibilities?

14. Which New Deal agencies were most beneficial to the interests of African Americans?

15. What were the causes of the Harlem riot of 1935?

16.   How did John L. Lewis and the CIO make labor unions attractive
       to black workers?

Identification Questions

You should be able to describe the following key terms, concepts,
individuals, and places and explain their significance:

1.   Friends of Negro Freedom
2.   National Association for the Promotion of Labor Unionism
3.   *Messenger*
4.   American Negro Labor Congress
5.   Angelo Herndon
6.   John J. Parker
7.   United Front Against Fascism
8.   Harold L. Ickes
9.   Reverend John H. Johnson

Essay Questions

1.   Discuss the history of the establishment of the Brotherhood of
      Sleeping Car Porters and Maids and explain why the creation of
      this labor union had such great significance for African Americans

2.   Describe the life of a black cotton or tobacco farmer in the South
      during the 1920s and 1930s and explain why his or her economic
      situation declined during these years.

3.   Explain why African Americans employed in the automobile and
      the food processing industries of the North were affected so
      immediately and so negatively at the onset of the Great Depression
      in 1929.

SELF-TEST

Multiple-Choice

1. Three of the following are true of Oscar DePriest. Which one is **not** true?
    a. His first elective office was that of Chicago alderman.
    b. He was elected to Congress in 1928.
    c. He was the first black Democrat ever to sit in Congress.
    d. His presence in Washington symbolized the regeneration of black Americans in politics.

2. Roosevelt's black advisors differed from earlier black presidential advisors in which of the following important respects?
    a. Their number was larger.
    b. They served in significant official positions.
    c. They were highly trained persons entrusted with specific functions to perform.
    d. All of the above are true.

3. All of the following are reasons that many southern white leaders found the New Deal distasteful except
    a. it concentrated too much power in Washington, DC.
    b. its relief and recovery programs were administered directly from Washington DC, with no implementation on the local level.
    c. it relieved the suffering of many of those on whose poverty some white politicians had climbed to power.
    d. it undertook to force equality in the administration of its benefits.

4. One reason Franklin D. Roosevelt succeeded in gaining a large following among blacks was that
   a. he refused to tolerate discrimination in the administration of New Deal relief programs.
   b. he dined with Booker T. Washington in the White House.
   c. blacks came to regard New Deal economic programs as especially beneficial to them.
   d. he established a "Negro Bureau" designed to deal with all matters affecting black people.

5. Mary McLeod Bethune served in what position in the Franklin D. Roosevelt administration?
   a. racial advisor in the Department of the Interior
   b. a special assistant to the U.S. Attorney General
   c. director of the Division of Negro Affairs of the National Youth Administration
   d. racial relations advisor in the Office of Civilian Defense

Fill-in-the-Blank

1. _____ were nine young African-American men who were unjustly arrested on rape charges in 1932; their subsequent conviction became a rallying point for civil rights advocates.

2. _____ founded the Congress of Industrial Organizations (CIO) and led efforts to extend unionization and union benefits to African Americans.

3. _____ was both the founder of the Brotherhood of Sleeping Car Porters and Maids and the copublisher of the *Messenger*.

4. One of the most outrageous abuses of African Americans was a United States Public Health Service study begun in 1932 and known as _____.

5. In 1935, the anger of African Americans toward white merchants and landlords led to a major riot in the black community of _____ in _____.

True/False

1. Oscar DePriest was the first black Democrat ever to sit in the United States Congress.

2. The Great Depression hit the black wage earner with particular severity.

3. From its beginning, the CIO sought to organize workers regardless of race or skill.

4. It was during World War I that African Americans forced open the door of the automobile industry.

5. Beginning around 1928, prominent African-American Republican leaders such as Benjamin Davis of Georgia, Perry Howard of Mississippi, and William McDonald of Texas gained even greater influence in the Republican Party in their states.

Relevance Today

1. During the Great Depression, blacks were discriminated against in the administration of relief. Today, has our nation eliminated discrimination in its programs to help citizens at time of crisis?

2. Blacks began to be drawn to the Democratic Party during the Franklin D. Roosevelt administration. What are the political loyalties of African Americans today? What are the reasons for them?

3.   President Franklin D. Roosevelt was a pioneer in appointing African Americans to positions in federal government departments. Are such appointments common today under both Democratic and Republican presidents?

4.   During the Great Depression, when some blacks were displeased by a lack of jobs and discrimination, they used what force they could command to demand and promote changes. What are the tactics used today by angry African Americans to demand and promote changes? Are they effective?

5.   The shift of many American labor unions toward the inclusion of black workers during the Great Depression was a great gain for African Americans. Are blacks today full participants in American labor unions?

CHAPTER 20
THE AMERICAN DILEMMA

THEMES AND MAJOR TOPICS

African Americans who migrated from rural areas to urban centers typically enjoyed better educational opportunities.

A persistent problem confronting African Americans was the disparity between the money spent for the education of white children and that spent on education for black children.

Segregated schools constituted a bulwark for white supremacy in the South.

Between 1945 and 1977, black college enrollment, as well as the number of African-American professors at white colleges and universities, increased steadily.

Years of legal challenges to institutionalized segregation in education culminated in the 1954 *Brown v. Topeka, Kansas, Board of Education* decision which declared segregated schools to be unconstitutional.

In addition to struggling both to survive and to assimilate into the larger American community, African Americans enhanced the quality of their lives through a variety of artistic and literary expressions.

Despite the enormous opportunities created for African Americans as a result of urbanization and industrialization, barriers between the races continued to sustain assumptions of African-American inferiority.

Lack of opportunities for African Americans to participate fully in the affairs of other institutions caused many to concentrate their energies on the church.

Through the creation of separate black associations for professional, religious, and social development, African Americans were able to wield influence not only in the African-American world but also in the larger American society.

KEY EVENTS

1870	Illiteracy rate for African Americans above ten years old was 81 percent.
1899	Supreme Court rendered decision in *Cumming v. The School Board of Richmond County, GA.*
1900	By 1900, every state in the South had enacted laws that provided for separate schools for blacks and whites. In 1900, for every $2 spent on the education of blacks in the South, $3 was spent on whites.
1916	The Association for the Study of Negro Life and History began publication of the *Journal of Negro History.*
1929–1941	Depression caused special hardships for southern schools for African Americans.
1930	Illiteracy rate for African Americans above ten years old dropped to 16 percent.
1935	Donald Murray, an African American, won his suit for admission to the University of Maryland Law School.
1936	National Negro Congress founded.

1937	Southern Negro Youth Congress founded.

1937   Southern Negro Youth Congress founded.

1938   On Easter Sunday, Marian Anderson, the great contralto, performed on the steps of the Lincoln Memorial. Hattie McDaniel won an Oscar for her role in *Gone with the Wind.*

1943   Thirty-three historically black institutions of higher education formed the United Negro College Fund.

1944   Black and white southerners established the Southern Regional Council. American Council on Race Relations founded.

1949   Ada Sipuel, an African American, won her suit for admission to the University of Oklahoma Law School.

1952   Ralph Ellison's *Invisible Man* won the National Book Award.

1954   On May 17 the U.S. Supreme Court outlaws segregation in its *Brown v. Topeka, Kansas, Board of Education* decision.

1965   Malcolm X assassinated.

1968   Martin Luther King, Jr., assassinated.

1970   There were 378,000 African Americans in predominantly white colleges and universities.

1977   There were 1.1 million African Americans in predominantly white colleges and universities, accounting for 9.3 percent of the nationwide enrollment.

1984   By 1984, the number of African Americans attending
institutions of higher education had dropped to 993,574; of
these, 267,000 were in historically black institutions, which
continued to provide more than half of all the bachelor's
degrees received by African Americans.

CHAPTER OVERVIEW

During the twentieth century, African Americans expressed an
intense desire for access to all levels of education, public and private.
Their educational progress could be seen in the following: steadily rising
rates of school attendance; dramatic increases in literacy; expansion in the
number of historically black educational institutions and the programs
they offered; a series of legal victories for African Americans in the South
who sued for admission to historically white educational institutions;
expanded access to libraries and organizations such as the Young Men's
Christian Association, the Young Women's Christian Association, the Boy
Scouts, and the Girl Scouts; a visible growth in the number of highly
trained African-American professionals; the establishment of several
influential scholarly journals within the black community; the expanding
readership of black newspapers and popular magazines; the growing
membership, influence, and wealth of many black religious communities;
the establishment of several new and influential black and interracial
organizations committed to promoting equal rights and racial harmony;
scholarly studies by highly respected scholars that began to challenge U.S.
citizens to face and resolve the "American Dilemma", new community
and educational programs that sought to address the needs of minority
youth; and, most important of all, the historic 1954 decision of the United
States Supreme Court outlawing segregation of schools in *Brown v.
Topeka, Kansas, Board of Education.*

Twentieth-century impediments to the progress of African
Americans included flagrantly discriminatory underfunding of black
education in the South; frequently segregated and often inadequate schools
for blacks in the South, North, and West; limited opportunities in most

fields of employment and areas of opportunity for all but the most talented and gifted of African Americans; the widespread refusal of many white Americans, especially those in southern states, to comply with the *Brown v. Topeka, Kansas, Board of Education* decision; and the destructive impact of negative conditions in urban environments on black individuals and their families.

Numerous talented young African Americans emerged as major figures in music—most notably, in jazz, gospel, the concert stage, and opera—and in literature as novelists, short story writers, poets, playwrights, and critics. Black American actors, however, had only the most limited access to the increasingly influential and highly lucrative medium of movies, where they were usually cast in stereotyped racial roles.

REVIEW QUESTIONS

Chapter Content Review

1. What was the decision of the United States Supreme Court in *Cumming v. The School Board of Richmond County, GA*? When was the decision handed down? How did it affect African Americans?

2. Who was Ambrose Caliver? What was his impact on the African-American community?

3. What were the three "general-types" of historically black colleges?

4. Who was the first African American to gain admission to the University of Maryland Law School? On what grounds did the Court decree admission?

5. What were the specifics in the United States Supreme Court's decision *in Missouri ex rel. Gaines v. Canada, Registrar of the University et al.*? When was the decision delivered?

6. What important strategic decision did the NAACP make in 1951 in regard to its campaign for equal rights for African Americans?

7. Name some of the scholarly journals established by African Americans and historically black colleges and universities during the twentieth century.

8. List some of the cities in which jazz flourished during the twentieth century. Who were some of the outstanding musicians in this field?

9. To whom is the success and popularity of gospel music during the 1930s and later largely attributed?

10. What were the events that led to a concert by Marian Anderson on the steps of the Lincoln Memorial on Easter Sunday 1939?

11. Who were Margaret Walker and Gwendolyn Brooks? What did they have in common?

12. What were the subjects of Richard Wright's books? Why is he considered to be such an important writer?

13. What is the Nation of Islam? What role did it play in twentieth-century African-American history?

14. Why did African Americans invest so much time and energy in their religious institutions? What were some of the tangible signs of the importance of churches to blacks? Why were African Americans so little interested in integrating their churches?

15. Why did the number of black newspapers and magazines increase rapidly after World War I?

16. What were the goals of the National Negro Congress and the Southern Negro Youth Congress? In what kinds of public activities did they engage to promote those goals?

17. What were the goals and activities of the Southern Conference for Human Welfare? How did it seek to promote the well-being of the African-American community?

18. In what part of the United States was the American Council on Race Relations active? What were its goals and activities?

19. Explain the differences and similarities among the following organizations and their programs: Operation Headstart, Higher Horizon, SEEK, and Access to Excellence.

Identification Questions

You should be able to describe the following key terms, concepts, individuals, and places and explain their significance:

1. Atlanta University System
2. United Negro College Fund
3. Marguerite Ross Barnett
4. Ada Sipuel
5. Ella Fitzgerald and Lena Horne
6. "Precious Lord, Take My Hand"
7. *Invisible Man*
8. *The Fire Next Time*
9. Malcolm X
10. National Negro Association
11. *Ebony, Jet, Tuesday,* and *Monitor*
12. Negro History Week

13. William Grant Still
14. Leontyne Price
15. James Baldwin
16. Ralph Ellison
17. Hattie McDaniel
18. Gunnar Myrdal

Essay Questions

1. Trace the history of the various legal decisions that made education more accessible to African Americans.

2. Discuss the ways in which the shift of many African Americans from the rural South to America's urban centers led to the creation of blacks' separate world within the cities of the United States.

3. Examine the conclusions of Gunnar Myrdal's 1944 study, *An American Dilemma,* and discuss whether they are still relevant or now irrelevant to black-white relations in twentieth-century America.

SELF-TEST

Multiple-Choice

1. Certain trends in the higher education of blacks became noticeable in the second half of the twentieth century. Which of these was **not** one of them?
   a. a dramatic increase in the enrollment of blacks in predominantly white colleges and universities
   b. a marked increase in the number of black administrators in black colleges
   c. a noticeable decrease in graduate and professional training of blacks
   d. an increase in the number of black administrators in predominantly white colleges

2. *Brown v. Topeka, Kansas, Board of Education* was concerned with
   a. equal rights for women.
   b. voting rights for black people.
   c. discrimination in the sale of housing.
   d. racial segregation in public schools.

3. By 1900, every state in the South had enacted laws that provided for
   a. free tuition grants to blacks enrolled in graduate programs in the region's public universities.
   b. separate black and white public schools.
   c. the admission of qualified black students to the predominantly white professional schools of the section.
   d. a system of integrated elementary schools.

4. African Americans turned to the church for
   a. self-expression.
   b. recognition.
   c. leadership.
   d. all of the above.

5. The Nation of Islam
   a. dramatically pointed out the theme of African-American alienation.
   b. sought assimilation.
   c. offered security and encouragement to unemployed and struggling African Americans.
   d. a and c.

6. The existence of a separate black community
   a. ensured the development of a black professional class.
   b. meant that adjustments to the larger society could not be made by the majority of blacks.
   c. meant that opportunities were greater.
   d. none of the above.

Fill-in-the-Blank

1. _____ was the founder of the Association for the Study of Negro Life and History.

2. _____ wrote the decision in the *Brown v. Topeka, Kansas, Board of Education* case.

3. _____ was the foundation that assisted in the construction of more than 5,000 school buildings for African Americans in fifteen states between 1913 and 1922.

4. _____ was an African-American writer who established himself as one of the major literary figures in the nation with such works as *Native Son* and *Black Boy*.

True/False

1. In the twentieth century, the interest of blacks in education noticeably declined.

2. African Americans obtained court support for their entrance into hitherto all-white southern graduate and professional schools.

3. Protests of African Americans against their status reflected a lack of pride in their race and its history.

4. James Baldwin and Richard Wright were two of the most prominent African-American musicians of the 1940s and 1950s.

5. Segregated schools operated only in the South between 1919 and 1941.

Relevance Today

1. Franklin and Moss indicate that there was scant opportunity for young African Americans to pursue acting careers, both during and after the Depression, because of the limitations placed upon blacks by the demands of the theatre-going public. Recently, Kweisi Mfume, head of the NAACP, has threatened to bring suit against television producers because of the lack of black actors and programs on major network television. To what extent should government intervene in society to alter public demand with respect to entertainment? Should production companies employ minority actors in proportion to their numbers in society, even if it means incurring economic losses?

2. A recurring theme in African-American history involves the tension generated by the requirement that African Americans live in two worlds at the same time. What are the advantages to living in only one world? In a country linked by so much media and technology, can an American today actually live in only one world? What are the advantages of being able to live in multiple worlds?

CHAPTER 21
FIGHTING FOR THE FOUR FREEDOMS

THEMES AND MAJOR POINTS

As the United States moved toward active participation in World War II, African Americans condemned the fascist movements that had come to power in Europe.

African Americans expressed outrage when the U.S. Department of War declared that blacks must serve in segregated military units and black officers would be limited in number and authority.

In a dramatic confrontation, the black March on Washington Movement forced President Franklin D. Roosevelt to issue Executive Order 8802, outlawing discrimination in defense and government employment.

Approximately a half million African Americans saw service overseas during World War II.

Because of the blatant racism African-American men and women in uniform experienced at home and in the battle theatres, the problem of maintaining high morale among them was very difficult. Nevertheless, many units and individuals received honors for their contribution to the victory of the United States and its allies.

African Americans on the "home front" vigorously supported the U.S. war effort, in spite of numerous clashes in employment settings with whites who resented them as coworkers and in residential areas where whites sought to drive out black homeowners and renters. For American blacks, World War II was a fight for "a double victory," better treatment at home as well as an overseas war against the United States' foreign enemies.

When the United States and its allies created the United Nations, American blacks hoped it would prove to be an ally in their fight for equal rights in their homeland.

KEY EVENTS

1935   Italy invaded Ethiopia.

1936   African-American Olympic medalists Jesse Owens and Ralph Metcalfe insulted by Hitler in Berlin.

1939   World War II began with Hitler's invasion of Poland.

1940   In September, black American leaders submitted a seven-point program to President Roosevelt outlining minimum essentials for giving African Americans just consideration in the defense program.
        In October, Colonel B. O. Davis became the first African American to be promoted to the rank of brigadier general.

1941   In January, A. Philip Randolph advocated a march on Washington.
        In June, President Roosevelt issued Executive Order 8802, banning discrimination in defense industries.
        On December 7, the Japanese attacked Pearl Harbor; Doris Miller, a black Navy messman, shot down four enemy planes.

1942   Approximately 370,000 African-American men entered the armed services.

1943   On June 20, the most serious domestic race riot of the World War II years began in Detroit.

1944   On July 8, the War Department issued an order forbidding racial segregation in its recreational and transportation facilities.

1945   World War II ended; approximately 1 million African-American men and women served in the U.S. Armed Forces during its duration.

1950   Ralph Bunche became the first African American to receive the Nobel Peace Prize for his work as a United Nations mediator in Palestine.

CHAPTER OVERVIEW

In the years leading up to the start of World War II, African Americans recognized that some of the world's most racist and antidemocratic forces were represented in the rise of fascism and nazism. From 1939, when the United States began to shift from an official position of neutrality to one of military preparedness and active support of the Allied Powers, to the close of World War II in 1945, blacks in America fought continuously for access to the various branches of the armed services, for the right to be trained and commissioned as officers, for equal and nondiscriminatory services in the military, and, equally important, for jobs in government agencies and employment sectors receiving federal funding. African Americans' greatest success in regard to fair employment came in 1941, when President Roosevelt issued Executive Order 8802 in response to the threat of a national demonstration by blacks against racism in the United States.

Although African Americans fought in segregated military units in World War II, their numbers steadily increased, and their treatment by whites in the services improved over the course of the war. When blacks received greater respect and better treatment, it was almost always the result of their outstanding military performance. Nevertheless, during the war years, there were numerous incidents of violence against black men and women in the service.

On the home front, there were numerous racial clashes as African Americans entered defense plants and communities where their presence was resented. For African Americans, World War II constituted a fight against oppression at home as well as abroad. When the conflict ended with the structure of Jim Crow segregation still intact in their country, black leaders turned to the newly formed United Nations as their best hope for help in fighting the forces of American racial prejudice.

REVIEW QUESTIONS

Chapter Content Review

1. How many African Americans served in the United States Army in 1940 and what were some of their units?

2. Did the Selective Service Act of 1940 initially promote the entrance of African Americans into the United States Army?

3. In September 1940, what requests did African-American leaders make of President Roosevelt?

4. Who was A. Philip Randolph and what was the "March on Washington" plan he conceived in January 1941? How was the plan received by African Americans and the Roosevelt administration? Did the plan produce any results?

5. What were the "Four Freedoms" to which President Roosevelt frequently made reference as America's wartime goals? What do you think were the differences and similarities between how black and white Americans understood the "Four Freedoms" to apply to their lives?

6. What were the events that made it possible for African Americans to serve as fighter pilots in World War II?

7.   What were the events that made it possible for African Americans to serve as officers in the United States Navy?

8.   When were officer candidate schools opened to African Americans? What was the rate of graduation of blacks from these schools? Were these officer candidate schools segregated?

9.   Why did the World War II service of the all black Ninety-Second Division become so controversial?

10. Why was it so difficult to maintain high morale among African Americans in the military services?

11. Who was Doris Miller? What services did he render for his country during World War II?

12. What were some of the major industries in which African Americans gained employment during World War II?

13. What were some of the distinct ways that African-American women supported the American war effort in the military services and on the home front?

14. Why did so many African Americans migrate to the North and West during World War II?

15. What was the date and the cause of the Detroit race riot during World War II?

Identification Questions

You should be able to describe the following key terms, concepts, individuals, and places and explain their significance:

1. Ethiopia
2. Executive Order 8802
3. 761st Tank Battalion
4. Ninety-Ninth Pursuit Squadron
5. Captain Hugh Mulzac
6. Private George Watson
7. Crystal Bird Fauset
8. Dr. Charles Drew
9. Ted Poston
10. *Negroes and the War*
11. United Nations
12. Jan Smuts
13. Ralph Bunche
14. Charles H. Houston

Essay Questions

1. Trace the history of the "March on Washington" movement led by A. Phillip Randolph.

2. Choose any branch of the United States Armed Forces that existed between 1940 and 1945 and do a history of the service of African-American men or women or both in that branch.

3. Do a history of the 1943 race riot in Detroit.

SELF-TEST

Multiple-Choice

1. During World War II, blacks for the first time were permitted to serve in the
   a. Marine Corps.
   b. infantry.
   c. signal corps.
   d. field artillery.

2. The most serious riot of the World War II period occurred in
   a. Los Angeles.
   b. Atlanta.
   c. Detroit.
   d. New York.

3. The director of the United Nations' Trusteeship Council and winner of the Nobel Peace Prize in 1950 was
   a. W.E.B. Du Bois.
   b. E. Franklin Frazier.
   c. Walter White.
   d. Ralph Bunche.

4. The conduct of African-American marines caused the commander of the corps to say that
   a. "the admission of blacks to the Marine Corps was a mistake."
   b. "the death rate of black marines was too high."
   c. "black marines were effective in the Pacific theatre but not in the European and North African theatres of war."
   d. "black marines were no longer on trial; they were marines, period."

5.	When the War Department forbade racial discrimination in recreational and transportation facilities in an order of July 8, 1944, an editorial in the Montgomery, Alabama, *Advertiser* said,
	a.	"At long last fairness for all our servicemen."
	b.	"Army orders, even armies, even bayonets, cannot force impossible and unnatural social relations upon us."
	c.	"God never intended for the races to mix together socially."
	d.	"Since all of America's servicemen are called upon to lay their lives on the line for the protection of their country, all of them should have access to their country's recreational and transportation facilities."

Fill-in-the-Blank

1.	_____'s threat to organize a massive protest march on Washington, DC, forced President Roosevelt to issue an executive order forbidding racial discrimination in employment in defense industries.

2.	The famous executive order referred to in #1 above was called _____.

3.	_____ was the first African American to obtain the rank of brigadier general in America's armed forces.

4.	Organized in San Francisco in 1945, the _____ is committed to the settlement of world problems and the maintenance of peace among nations.

5.	During World War II, African-American women gained admission to the _____.

True/False

1. Because it did not directly affect them, African Americans failed to condemn the fascist movement in Europe.

2. Job discrimination in the defense industry was eliminated by the Committee on Fair Employment Practices.

3. The "Double-V" campaign stood for victory over the Germans as well as over the Japanese.

4. In the early 1990s, when the army initiated a study to "determine why no black had received the Medal of Honor" in World War II, it concluded no African American had qualified.

5. The 1943 race riot in Detroit was brought to a halt by the successful efforts of the city's white civic, political, and religious leaders to get the rioters to lay down their arms and discuss the tensions that had produced the clash.

Relevance Today

1. On the eve of World War II, African Americans sought improvements in their treatment by whites. Blacks did this in the belief that only while powerful whites needed black support in the coming war would they respond to African-American demands for fairness. Do blacks and other disadvantaged minorities today continue to believe that those who hold power in America care about them only when they need the support of minorities to promote their own well-being?

2. Despite racism, the African-American men and women who served in World War II fought courageously for the United States. Do you believe, as many blacks and whites do, that at present the U.S. military forces have done more than any other important American

institution to eliminate bias and guarantee equal opportunities for all who serve in them?

3. In spite of the many problems blacks faced during World War II, developments in the United States and abroad gave them hope for the future. Do you see the fulfillment of those hopes in the situation of African Americans living in the United States today?

CHAPTER 22
AFRICAN AMERICANS IN THE COLD WAR ERA

THEMES AND MAJOR TOPICS

- World War II created a climate that permitted substantial economic, social, and political gains for African Americans. Leadership exercised after the war by black organizations, and the executive and judicial branches of government, shattered many of the impediments to racial equality in America.

- Black political power increased substantially after the war, as African-American migration to western and northern industrial centers led to more electoral clout.

- With the increase in black economic and political power came intensified efforts by whites—e.g., White Citizens Councils—to obstruct desegregation and block any measure or effort intended to secure African-American freedom.

- American racial policies during the Cold War made political leaders sensitive to Soviet charges that America was both corrupt and hypocritical.

- The urban ghetto, replete with its widespread socioeconomic problems, became a permanent fixture in America by the time of the Cold War.

- During the Cold War, many African-American religious leaders exerted authority in a wide range of arenas.

KEY EVENTS

1946   Harry S. Truman appointed a presidential commission on
              civil rights, which issued the report *To Secure These
              Rights.*

1947   Jackie Robinson signed by the Brooklyn Dodgers as the
              first African-American player in major league baseball.

1948   Harry S Truman appointed a presidential commission on
              race relations in the armed forces, which issued the report
              Freedom to Serve.
              President Truman issued an executive order forbidding
              discrimination in the hiring policies of the federal
              government.
              The U.S. Supreme Court outlawed restrictive covenants.

1949   Following the recommendations of *Freedom to Serve,* the
              United States began to integrate its armed forces.

1950–1951   United States forces fighting in the Korean War became the
              first integrated American army in U.S. history.

1950   The U.S. Supreme Court ruled that segregation of African
              Americans on dining cars of interstate railroads is illegal.
              Professional basketball and tennis integrated with the
              admission of African-American players to teams and
              tournaments.

1952   A majority of African-American voters supported the
              losing Democratic candidate, Adlai Stevenson, in the
              presidential election.

1953   E. Frederick Morrow appointed administrative assistant in
              the executive offices of the president of the United States.

1954	Three African Americans, all Democrats, elected to the United States House of Representatives.
1955	The Interstate Commerce Commission decreed all racial segregation on interstate trains and buses must end January 10, 1956. Near Greenwood, Mississippi, Emmett Till, a fourteen-year-old African American was murdered for allegedly whistling at a white woman.
1956	The African-American communities of Montgomery, Alabama, and Tallahassee, Florida, began a boycott of their respective city bus lines to secure better treatment and services for black patrons. The governors of South Carolina, Georgia, Mississippi, and Virginia called on southern states to declare that the federal government has no power to prohibit segregation and to protest the "encroachment" of the federal government on the "sovereignty" of the states. Ninety southern members of Congress issued their "declaration of constitutional principals," commonly known as the "Southern Manifesto." Several southern states passed laws to stop the operation of the NAACP within their borders. A federal court ordered Alabama to admit Autherine Lucy, an African-American applicant, to the University of Alabama. Nat "King" Cole, an African-American singer, briefly hosted his own television show.
1963	Sidney Poitier, an African American, won an Oscar as best actor for his performance in *Lilies of the Field*.
1964	Six African Americans elected to the United States House of Representatives.

1965	Carl Rowan, an African American, began to write a syndicated column and to appear on national radio and television as a commentator.
1966	Bill Cosby, an African American, received an Emmy Award for his role in the television series *I Spy*.
1968	Congress passed the Fair Housing Act, barring racial discrimination in the sale, rental, or financing of most housing units.
1970	A sharp rise in the number of black female-headed families began—an indication of the pressures weakening the African-American family. Maya Angelou wrote *I Know Why the Caged Bird Sings*.
1970–1974	*The Flip Wilson Show,* the first variety show hosted by an African American, was consistently rated among the top programs on television.
1974	Max Robinson, an African American, became a national anchorman for the *ABC Evening News*.
1976	Ntozake Shange wrote *For Colored Girls Who Have Considered Suicide/When the Rainbow Is Enuf*.
1977	Millions of American viewers saw Alex Haley's *Roots,* a television mini-series.
1978	James A. McPherson's *Elbow Room* won the Pulitzer Prize for fiction. Boxer Muhammad Ali (Cassius Clay) once again won the crown as world heavyweight champion. He lost the title several years earlier, when he was found guilty of violating the Selective Service Act.

1980	Robert L. Johnson established the Black Entertainment Network (BET) as part of the cable television system.
1982	Alice Walker's *The Color Purple* received the Pulitzer Prize.
1983	About 48 percent of all black children under eighteen lived in female-headed households.
	Bryant Gumbel selected to co-host NBC's *Today Show.*
1985	Oprah Winfrey began her television program, *The Oprah Winfrey Show.*
1986	Spike Lee produced *She's Gotta Have It.*
	Charlayne Hunter-Gault became a regular correspondent on *The MacNeil-Lehrer News Hour.*
1988	Toni Morrison's *Beloved* won the Pulitzer Prize.
1989	Bernard Shaw became the principal anchor in Washington, DC, for the Cable News Network (CNN).
1992	Spike Lee produced *Malcolm X.*
1993	Rita Dove became the youngest U.S. poet laureate.
	William A. Hilliard, editor of the *Portland Oregonian,* elected as first black president of the American Society of Newspaper Editors.
	Bob Herbert joined the *New York Times* as the first African-American columnist on its Opinion and Editorial page.

CHAPTER OVERVIEW

During the three decades after World War II, the general situation of the African-American community steadily improved economically, politically, and socially. Blacks, their hopes and ambitions stimulated by the vision of freedom proclaimed in wartime propaganda, pressed both individually and through their racial institutions to push the doors of equality and opportunity ever wider. Their successful efforts were assisted frequently by strategic support from a broad range of predominately white organizations committed to reforming race relations in the United States. The courts, chiefly but not exclusively the federal ones, increasingly took cognizance of racial questions and frequently ruled in favor of equality. The executive branch of the federal government, moreover, sensitive to both domestic and foreign pressures, exerted considerable influence in eradicating the gap between creed and practice in America.

The improvement of the status of African Americans, however, was neither uniform nor without vigorous opposition in some quarters. In the southern states, African Americans faced white resistance to integration in the form of economic reprisals, violence from officers of the law as well as from extra-legal vigilante groups, and public political opposition from most elected officials in the region. Parts of the South saw the amount of violence rise to proportions of a reign of terror.

Throughout the United States, responsible citizens, concerned about mounting racial tension, called for federal action, but neither the president nor the Congress seemed inclined to intervene. One of the most dramatic facts of life for black Americans in the Cold War era was their continuing urbanization. This was directly responsible for many of the positive changes, particularly the growing political strength of African-American voters, and the willingness of the two major political parties to court those voters by rhetorical and sometimes actual support of efforts to secure equal rights for blacks.

There were, however, significant negative aspects to urbanization. In many instances, the arrival of blacks in the central cities of the United States caused whites to depart, taking with them most employment opportunities that blacks sought. The black ghetto that had become a fixture in urban America earlier in the twentieth century gained a measure of permanence during the black migration of the World War II and postwar years, as most blacks found it very nearly impossible to purchase or rent in predominantly white communities. Perhaps the most troubling development was the dramatic deterioration of the black family, most graphically reflected in the sharp rise in the number of African-American female-headed households beginning in the 1960s and accelerating in the 1970s.

By contrast, the African Americans who benefited most from expanded opportunities made possible the revitalization and expansion of black religious institutions, the growth in circulation and influence of black newspapers and magazines, and the expanded presence of blacks in various new and old businesses that served the African-American community and in predominantly white business enterprises. For Americans of all races, expanded opportunity for African Americans was demonstrated by the fame and, in some instances, the large financial rewards that came to the talented blacks whose achievements made them prominent in literature, the arts, music, journalism, theatre, films, sports, and television.

REVIEW QUESTIONS

Chapter Content Review

1.   What specific actions did President Harry S. Truman take to promote equality for African Americans?

2.   How did the decisions of courts during the Cold War era affect the status and treatment of African Americans?

3.   During what war did the United States deploy its first integrated army?

4.   Who was the first African-American player in Major League baseball?

5.   Who were the two African Americans elected national officers of the AFL-CIO in 1955? What was the importance of this event?

6.   What was the name of the fourteen-year-old African American killed in Mississippi in 1955? What was the alleged cause of his murder?

7.   In what two cities did African Americans begin a boycott of the city bus lines to secure better treatment and service for black patrons? What year did the boycotts begin?

8.   What was the "Southern Manifesto"?

9.   By 1980, did the majority of African Americans live in urban or rural areas? What were the percentages?

10.   When did observers begin to notice the rise within the African-American community of female-headed families? Why was this so troubling?

Identification Questions

You should be able to describe the following key terms, concepts, individuals, and places and explain their significance:

1.   *Freedom to Serve*
2.   Autherine Lucy
3.   Willard Townsend
4.   J. Watie Waring

5. Rita Dove
6. William Hilliard
7. Highlander Folk School
8. Chicago *Defender*
9. North Carolina Mutual Life Insurance Company
10. Elizabeth Catlett
11. Andre Watts

Essay Questions

1. Trace the history of Harry S. Truman's support of black civil rights while in the White House. Discuss how he became interested in civil rights and what the ultimate goals of his civil rights policies were.

2. Present a history of the integration of African-American players into professional baseball.

3. Present a history of the resistance to racial integration of any one of the southern states that practiced legal segregation during the Cold War era.

SELF-TEST

Multiple-Choice

1. Which of the following was the last branch of the federal government to move actively in the area of civil rights for blacks?
    a. the executive
    b. the legislative
    c. the judicial

2. Economic actions invoked against blacks who were active in civil rights in the 1950s included
   a. dismissals from jobs.
   b. denials of loans.
   c. foreclosures of mortgages.
   d. all of the above.

3. Southern white leaders fought school desegregation in several ways. Which of these was **not** one of them?
   a. turning schools over to private organizations
   b. encouraging "voluntary segregation"
   c. threatening to secede from the Union
   d. adopting "freedom of choice" plans

4. Some of the signs that the assault on discrimination and segregation was yielding results were evident in
   a. public housing.
   b. employment opportunities in numerous industries.
   c. the hiring of blacks as clerks, bookkeepers, and buyers in retail establishments.
   d. all of the above.

5. President Truman
   a. issued an executive order requiring fair employment in the federal service without regard to race, color, religion, or national origin.
   b. disappointed many African Americans because of his reluctance to deal with issues of race.
   c. was reluctant to issue an executive order requiring fair employment in the federal service because he feared losing southern support.
   d. did not agree that the full force and power of the federal government should be used to end racial discrimination.

Fill-in-the-Blank

1. _____ was the name of the presidential report that called for positive programs to strengthen civil rights.

2. _____ and _____ were the two African Americans elected vice president of the labor organization formed by the merger of the AFL and CIO.

3. _____ was the federal district judge who, in 1947, decided that African Americans could not be excluded from the Democratic primary in South Carolina.

4. The statement _____, issued by southern Congressmen following the *Brown v. Topeka, Kansas, Board of Education* decision of 1954, encouraged southerners to use "every lawful means" to resist the school desegregation decision.

5. _____ was and remains the most successful publishing venture in the history of black journalism.

True/False

1. President Truman contributed to the creation of a climate in which the status of blacks was officially degraded.

2. A battlefield test of armed forces integration received its first widespread application in Korea.

3. The political influence of African Americans increased substantially in the post-World War II decades.

4. Southern resistance to any change in the status of African Americans often degenerated into violence.

5. The first African-American Major League baseball player was Jack Johnson.

Relevance Today

1. In response to both the *Brown* decision in 1954 and the Supreme Court's order for the states to desegregate "with all deliberate speed," southern Congressmen signed the "Southern Manifesto," a document which condemned the decision and urged that it be resisted by "all legal means." Massive white resistance—violent, illegal, and rampant—followed. Do you believe that religious and political leaders act irresponsibly when they use inflammatory and divisive language? Do you believe elected officials have an obligation to represent, first and foremost, people of their own ethnic or racial group?

2. Whereas state and local laws mandated southern segregation prior to 1964, many unwritten policies and practices of empowered whites sustained segregation in the North. Consider the extent of segregation that exists in your own social context today: family, friends, school, community, place of work, or place of worship. Does the segregation arise naturally from the social organizations to which you or others belong? At what point in time does social segregation become harmful to society?

CHAPTER 23
THE BLACK REVOLUTION

THEMES AND MAJOR POINTS

Many factors stimulated African Americans to take direct and more drastic action to secure their full rights as citizens of the United States. Few, if any, were more important than the widespread, massive resistance of whites to the extension of those rights.

The sit-in movement launched by four black students was the beginning of the most profound, revolutionary changes in the status of African Americans that had occurred since emancipation.

As the Civil Rights Movement, dominated by the leadership and rhetoric of Martin Luther King, Jr., gathered power and momentum, African Americans and their allies discovered that large-scale demonstrations for equal rights, which frequently met the resistance of white segregationists, often accomplished what other measures had not.

With the vigorous support of President Lyndon B. Johnson, the United States Congress passed the Civil Rights Act of 1964 and the Voting Rights Act of 1965, which Johnson quickly signed. While these new federal laws give African Americans the illusion of equality, the day-to-day economic, educational, political, and social problems faced by blacks made it evident that much more needed to be done if black Americans were to enjoy equality.

As the 1960s drew to a close, the optimism generated in the African-American community by the Civil Rights Movement gave way to pessimism and even cynicism. These negative emotions were fed by bitter white resistance to racial change in every part of the country; the assassinations of Martin Luther King, Jr., and Malcolm X; and the demise of the Black Panther Party as an effective radical organization.

By the mid-1970s, the African-American community seemed to be dividing into two divergent groups: one consisting of trained and educated blacks who were experiencing unprecedented job opportunities that were at least comparable to those of white with equal qualifications, the other made up of a poor black underclass falling further and further behind other Americans in all the skills and qualities needed to succeed in a society growing even more competitive.

KEY EVENTS

1957	Governor Orval Faubus of Arkansas actively opposed the desegregation of Central High School in Little Rock. At President Eisenhower's initiative, the Congress passed a civil rights law.
1960	On February 1, four students from the North Carolina Agricultural and Technical College in Greensboro conducted the first major civil rights "sit-in" of the decade. There were more than 1 million registered African-American voters in twelve southern states; in at least six of the eight most populous states in the country, blacks held the balance of power in closely contested elections. John F. Kennedy's close victory over Richard M. Nixon in the presidential election was aided greatly by Kennedy's receipt of the majority of the African-American vote.
1960–1961	Strong protests in New Rochelle, New York; Englewood, New Jersey; Chester, Pennsylvania; and Chicago, Illinois occurred against school segregation in the North.
1961	In May, the Congress of Racial Equality (CORE) sent "freedom riders" into the South to test segregation laws and practices in interstate transportation.

1962	By 1962, more than thirty cases had been initiated by U.S. Attorney General Robert Kennedy to protect blacks in their efforts to vote in Mississippi, Louisiana, Alabama, Tennessee, and Georgia.
	In the face of serious opposition and with federal intervention, James Meredith was admitted to the University of Mississippi.
1963	Governor George Wallace was unable to block the enrollment of an African-American student at the University of Alabama.
	Medgar Evers, the leader of the Mississippi NAACP, was assassinated outside his home in Jackson.
	On August 28, 1963, as part of the "March on Washington for Jobs and Freedom," Martin Luther King, Jr., delivered his "I Have a Dream" speech.
	On November 22, President Kennedy was assassinated in Dallas.
1964	In January, the Twenty-Fourth Amendment to the Constitution, outlawing the poll tax, was ratified.
	In June, the Civil Rights Act of 1964 was passed by Congress.
	Fannie Lou Hamer addressed the Democratic National Convention as part of an effort to replace the all-white Mississippi delegation with the integrated Mississippi Freedom Democratic Party delegation.
	George Wallace, the segregationist governor of Alabama, made a strong showing in the presidential primaries of Wisconsin, Indiana, and Maryland.
	During the summer, major eruptions of racial violence, rioting, and looting occurred in New York City; Rochester, New York; Patterson, Elizabeth, and Jersey City, all in the state of New Jersey; Philadelphia; and Chicago.
	In November, the vast majority of African-American voters cast their ballots for the winning Democratic ticket of

Lyndon B. Johnson and Hubert H. Humphrey. By an overwhelming vote, California voters adopted a constitutional amendment guaranteeing a property owner the right to dispose of his or her property to anyone he or she chooses. In 1966, the California Supreme Court declared this amendment unconstitutional.

Less than 2 percent of the African-American students in the eleven states of the former Confederacy were in desegregated schools.

1965	President Johnson appointed Robert Weaver secretary of the New Department of Housing and Urban Development, making Weaver the first African American to hold a cabinet office. Martin Luther King, Jr., received the Nobel Peace Prize. In February, a young civil rights worker and a young white minister from Boston were killed in Selma, Alabama. To protest these events. Martin Luther King, Jr., led an interracial march from Selma to Montgomery. Snipers murdered a white woman from Detroit who participated in the march. At the urging of President Johnson, Congress passed the Voting Rights Act. In August, the predominately black Watts area of Los Angeles erupted in a major race riot. Malcom X was killed in New York City.
1965–1966	In the eleven southern states of the former Confederacy, 6 percent of African-American children attended desegregated schools.
1966	Stokely Carmichael, the new chairman of the Student Nonviolent Coordinating Committee (SNCC), urged the use of "black power" to combat "white power."
1967	President Johnson appointed Thurgood Marshall as the first African American to serve on the Supreme Court.

The Black Power Conference in Newark, New Jersey, called for the "partitioning of the United States into two separate independent nations, one to be a homeland for white and the other to be a homeland for black Americans." A group of young militants in California led by Huey P. Newton and Bobby Seale organized the Black Panther Party.

1968   On April 4, Martin Luther King, Jr., was killed in Memphis. In more than 100 cities, several days of rioting, burning, and looting ensued.
About 20 percent of the African-American schoolchildren in the former Confederate states were in "fully integrated schools."
The report of the National Advisory Commission on Civil Disorders stated that "our nation is moving toward two societies, one black, one white—separate and unequal."

1969   The Black Economic Development Conference met in Detroit and called upon the "White Christian Churches and the Jewish Synagogues and all other Racist Institutions" to pay "$500 million in reparations and to surrender 60 percent of their assets to be used for economic, social, and cultural rehabilitation of the black community."

1971   President Richard M. Nixon warned federal officials to stop pressing for desegregation of southern schools through "forced busing."
Shirley Chisholm conducted an unsuccessful campaign for the Democratic presidential nomination.

1973   The National Black Feminist Organization was founded.

1976   More than 90 percent of all black voters supported Jimmy Carter, the winning Democratic presidential candidate.

| 1978 | The Supreme Court ruled in the *Bakke* case that the factor of race alone could not be used to guarantee the admission of a certain number of blacks to a public medical college in California. |

More than 90 percent of the school systems in the South were classified as desegregated.

| 1983 | Guion S. Bluford became the first African-American astronaut. |

| 1992 | Mae E. Jemison became the first female African-American astronaut. |

CHAPTER OVERVIEW

Between 1960 and 1980, large numbers of African Americans resorted to direct action in order to secure for themselves the rights of American citizens. The widespread, massive, official, and unofficial resistance of whites to the extension of these rights to African Americans was one of the great stimulants to black activism. In many southern communities, economic sanctions were invoked against blacks who were active in civil rights, including dismissal from jobs, denial of loans, and foreclosure of mortgages. When these measures were ineffective, violence, including murder, was frequently used.

Throughout the United States, but especially in the South, the response of African Americans and their allies to opponents of civil rights and desegregation took the forms of boycotts, political action, sit-ins, voter-registration drives, freedom rides, freedom marches, and lobbying for new laws to guarantee protection of civil rights by the local, state, and federal government. In all these efforts, the growing size and political clout of black urban communities, North, South, and West, caused the major political parties to pay attention to black concerns and in some instances to promote them. The efforts of African Americans to secure their rights and the desire of the great majority of Americans for racial peace helped to make possible the passage of the Federal Civil Rights Act of 1964 and the Federal Voting Rights Acts of 1965.

As the Civil Rights Movement gained momentum, many of its supporters came to see it not only as an effort to obtain political equality for African Americans but also as a campaign for black economic equality, particularly in the areas of housing and employment. The inability, however, of the Civil Rights Movement to effectively promote changes in white attitudes and behavior that would guarantee economic equality for the majority of African Americans was directly responsible for the enhanced appeal of the Black Muslims, the Black Power Movement, and the Black Panther Party. The most negative statements of black disappointment and hopelessness in this regard were the urban riots of the 1960s and 1970s. And the belief of numerous female participants in the Civil Rights Movement that most of the movement's male leaders were sexist produced some of the earliest forms of individual and organized black feminism.

REVIEW QUESTIONS

Chapter Content Review

1.   What states passed fair employment laws between 1945 and 1959?

2.   Name the governor of Arkansas who opposed the desegregation of Little Rock's Central High School in 1957?

3.   What country became the first former African colony to join the United Nations? On what date did this occur?

4.   In what year did the Greensboro, North Carolina, "sit-in" action to promote civil rights for African Americans take place? Who were the individuals that initiated it?

5.   In what northern cities did major protests against school segregation take place in the years 1960 and 1961?

6.   What was the name of the organization which sent "freedom riders" into the South in 1961?

7.   How far had desegregation of schools in southern and border states proceeded by 1961?

8.   Describe the ruling handed down on September 22, 1961, by the United States Interstate Commerce Commission regarding segregation.

9.   What was the content of the executive order issued in 1962 by President John F. Kennedy in regard to discrimination and housing?

10.   Who was the first African American admitted to the University of Mississippi? In what year did the admission take place?

11.   Name the governor of Alabama who sought in 1963 to block the admission of an African American to his state's university.

12.   Name the leader of the NAACP in Mississippi who was shot outside his home in 1963.

13.   What was the date, place, and occasion on which Martin Luther King, Jr., delivered his famous address on civil rights in the United States? What was the title of the address?

14.   Name and describe two decisions of the United States Supreme Court in 1963 that strengthened the resolve of civil rights activists.

15.   Describe the Twenty-Fourth Amendment to the United States Constitution. Give the year it was ratified.

16. Give a general description of the Civil Rights Act of 1964.

17. Who was Fannie Lou Hamer? What did she attempt to do at the Democratic National Convention in 1964?

18. Who was George Wallace? What important victories did he achieve in the presidential primaries in 1964?

19. What amendment to the Constitution of the state of California was adopted by voters in 1964? How did the Supreme Court of California treat a challenge to this amendment in 1966?

20. Who was the first African American to be appointed to the presidential cabinet? In what year did the appointment take place? To what post was this individual appointed?

21. What major international award did Martin Luther King, Jr., receive in 1965?

22. What events promoted a major civil rights march from Selma to Montgomery in the state of Alabama in 1965?

23. Give a general description of the Voting Rights Act of 1965.

24. What major American city experienced a devastating race riot in 1965?

25. Name the black civil rights leader killed in New York City in 1965.

26. How far had the desegregation of southern schools progressed by 1966?

27. Who became chairperson of the Student Nonviolent Coordinating Committee (SNCC) in 1966? What new tactic did this individual advocate for the promotion of African-American equality?

28. How many African Americans were members of the Congress of the United States in 1966?

29. What new organization to promote African-American equality was founded in 1967? Who were its founders?

30. When and where was Martin Luther King, Jr., killed? What were the immediate consequences of his death?

31. How far had school desegregation progressed in the southern states by 1968?

32. What was the demand made by the Black Economic Development Conference on America's all-white and predominantly white religious institutions in 1969?

33. What was the approximate size of the Black Muslim community by the early 1970s?

34. What warning did President Richard M. Nixon issue to federal officials in 1971 concerning the use of busing to promote desegregation of schools?

35. Who was the first African-American woman to campaign for the Democratic presidential nomination? In what year did she seek it?

36. What presidential candidate did most African-American voters support in 1976?

37. What was the decision of the United States Supreme court in the *Bakke* case? In what year was the decision rendered?

38. What was the level of desegregation in southern public schools in 1978?

39. Name the major American cities that had African-American mayors in 1979.

40. Name the first African-American male astronaut and the first African-American female astronaut. In what year or years did each take his or her first flight?

41. In what major cities did major race riots occur?

Identification Questions

You should be able to describe the following key terms, concepts, individuals, and places and explain their significance:

1. Orval Faubus
2. Ghana
3. sit-in
4. freedom riders
5. James Meredith
6. George Wallace
7. Medgar Evers
8. Cambridge, Maryland
9. "I Have a Dream"
10. *Edwards v. South Carolina*
11. *Johnson v. Virginia*
12. Twenty-Fourth Amendment
13. Civil Rights Act of 1964
14. Fannie Lou Hamer
15. Council of Federated Organizations
16. Robert Weaver
17. Selma to Montgomery March
18. Voting Rights Act of 1965
19. Watts
20. Malcolm X
21. Stokely Carmichael

22. *United States v. Jefferson County*
23. Black Power Conference of 1967
24. Huey P. Newton and Bobby Seale
25. April 4, 1968
26. National Advisory Commission on Civil Disorders
27. Black Economic Development Conference
28. Shirley Chisholm
29. Yvonne Braithwaite Burke
30. National Black Organization
31. Barbara Jordan
32. Louis Martin
33. Guion S. Bluford
34. Mae E. Jemison

Essay Questions

1. Compare and contrast the presidential records of Dwight D. Eisenhower, John F. Kennedy, Lyndon B. Johnson, and Richard M. Nixon in regard to support for equal rights for African Americans.

2, Do a history of the "sit-in" launched in 1960 by the four African-American students at North Carolina Agricultural and Technical College in Greensboro. Be sure to explain why they risked their lives and futures in this way.

3. Discuss the differences and similarities between the tactics of Martin Luther King, Jr., and Malcolm X, as well as the influence each had on African Americans and other Americans.

4. Examine the ways in which the Black Power Movement turned the Civil Rights Movement in a new direction. Assess whether the overall impact of the Black Power Movement was good or bad.

SELF-TEST

Multiple-Choice

1. In 1960, four students from North Carolina Agricultural and Technical University
    a. inaugurated a back-to-Africa Movement.
    b. issued a Black Power manifesto.
    c. declared the south an unfit region for African Americans.
    d. launched a "sit-in" movement.

2. During his years as president of the United States, John F. Kennedy
    a. secured passage of tough new civil rights laws by the United States Congress.
    b. made no appointments of African Americans to important federal offices.
    c. sought to elevate black Americans through expanded executive action and moral leadership.
    d. refused to take any active role in efforts to secure James Meredith's admission to the University of Mississippi.

3. The Watts riot occurred in
    a. New Orleans.
    b. Chicago.
    c. Las Vegas.
    d. Los Angeles.

4. The Black Panther Party for Self-Defense advocated
    a. the creation of one or more all-black states in the United States.
    b. nonviolence as the chief tactic of the Civil Rights Movement.
    c. total liberty for black Americans or total destruction for America.

5.   When the National Black Feminist Organization was founded in 1973, its leaders declared that
     a.   most Americans expect "black women to suppress their aspirations in deference to black males."
     b.   the new organization would make it clear to "the black liberation movement there can't be liberation for half a race."
     c.   "in many respects it was more difficult to be a woman than a black."
     d.   all of the above.

Fill-in-the-Blank

1.   The _____ Amendment outlawed the requirement of the poll tax, long a means of disenfranchising African Americans in federal elections.

2.   Appointed an Associate Justice of the United States Supreme Court, _____ was the first African American to occupy a seat on that bench.

3.   _____ is a kind of segregation resulting from the concentration of blacks in certain well-defined geographic areas, rather than from statutory regulation.

4.   In 1978, the U.S. Supreme Court ruled in the _____ case that the factor of race along could not be used to guarantee the admission of a certain number of blacks to a public medical college in California.

5.   In 1972, _____, a distinguished and articulate African-American congresswoman, campaigned for the Democratic presidential nomination.

True/False

1. President Kennedy's religion made him unacceptable to the vast majority of black voters.

2. The term *nonviolence* is closely associated with the early years of the Black Revolution.

3. A combination of executive action and federal legislation was successful in preventing the outbreak of racial violence in the mid-1960s.

4. In the presidential election of 1976, more than 90 percent of all black voters supported Jimmy Carter, the nominee of the Democratic Party.

5. During the 1970s, the two best known members of the Black Muslims, a vocal and vigorous religious community, were Elijah Muhammad and Muhammad Ali, formerly Cassius Clay.

Relevance Today

1. During the Civil Rights Movement, white resistance to the extension of equal rights to blacks stimulated African Americans to take direct and drastic action to secure their full rights. How do blacks fight to secure full rights today?

2. The sit-in movement launched by four black students was one of the most significant developments in the Civil Rights Movement. What role in promoting positive social change do students in the United States play today?

3. During the civil rights era, Americans of all races learned that laws do not make people equal in all ways. What allows a second-class citizen to become a first-class citizen in the United States today?

4.   At the close of the 1960s, African Americans were pessimistic, some even cynical, about their ability to attain equal rights in the United States. Do African Americans today feel more positive about their chances to achieve equality with white Americans?

5.   By the mid-1970s, the African-American community seemed to be splitting into a middle class and an underclass. Has this division disappeared, softened, or grown stronger?

CHAPTER 24
REACTION AND PROGRESS

THEMES AND MAJOR POINTS

- Ronald Reagan's attempts to both weaken enforcement of civil rights laws and dismantle programs that served African-American economic interests were roundly denounced by black leaders.

- The economic gap between the rich and the poor grew significantly during the Reagan and Bush years.

- Jesse Jackson's candidacy for the Democratic nomination for president in 1992 and 1996 stimulated minority participation and enthusiasm for electoral politics in the United States.

- Between 1970 and 1985 the number of black elected officials climbed from 1,469 to 6,056.

- Chief Justice William Rehnquist, along with Reagan appointees Anthony Scalia and Anthony Kennedy, played a crucial role in reversing civil rights gains that had been made in the 1970s.

- While predominantly white colleges and universities of the 1980s and 1990s strove to increase both minority enrollment and the hiring of minority leaders and professors, initiatives like Proposition 209 in California undermined race-specific programs that could benefit African Americans.

- Since the 1970s, black entertainers, media personalities, artists, and athletes have come to enjoy increasing recognition, success, and wealth in the United States.

KEY EVENTS

1980   Ronald Reagan was elected president by an enormous majority; 90 percent of the African-American vote went to the defeated Jimmy Carter.

1981   On January 15, 100,000 marchers converged on Washington, DC, to rally for a national holiday for Martin Luther King, Jr.

1982   The African-American unemployment rate was 18.9 percent, more than twice the white rate of 8.4 percent.

1983   In October, Jesse Jackson announced his candidacy for the Democratic nomination for president.
On November 2, President Ronald Reagan signed the bill establishing a national holiday in honor of Martin Luther King, Jr.

1985   While the African-American unemployment rate was 16.3 percent, the unemployment rate for whites was 6.2 percent; at the same time, the unemployment rate for young blacks (sixteen to nineteen) soared to more than 50 percent for the first time in history.

1988   For the second time, Jesse Jackson announced his candidacy for the presidential nomination of the Democratic Party.
George Bush was elected president, while 90 percent of the African-American community cast their votes for the losing Democratic candidate, Michael Dukakis.

1989   George Bush appointed Colin Powell to the most important military post ever occupied by an African American, chairman of the Joint Chiefs of Staff.

1991   Clarence Thomas was nominated to the United States Supreme Court by President Bush and confirmed by the United States Senate.

1992   In April, after the Los Angeles police officers who arrested
       Rodney King were acquitted of the charge of using "excessive
       force," Los Angeles erupted into four days of rioting, looting, and
       burning.
       In November, the Democratic presidential ticket of Bill Clinton
       and Albert Gore won election; 83 percent of the African-American
       vote went to Clinton and Gore.
       Carol Moseley-Braun of Illinois was elected to the U.S. Senate and
       became the first African-American woman to serve in that body.

CHAPTER OVERVIEW

In 1980, Ronald Reagan won the presidency of the United States with an overwhelming victory. Ninety percent of the African-American vote, however, went to his Democratic opponent, James Earl Carter, as it had four years earlier. Whether justified or not, African Americans were deeply distrustful of Reagan's intentions toward them. During the eight years he held office, these negative perceptions grew stronger for a number of reasons. Despite Reagan's choice of an African American as secretary of Housing and Urban Development, blacks were disappointed that so few members of their race received appointments. And, as the president initiated policies and measures that reflected his goals, most African Americans saw them as evidence that the Reagan administration had little or no commitment to supporting racial diversity in government: it was opposed to the implementation of voting rights, school desegregation, equal employment opportunity, and affirmative action; it was committed to weakening the force of the Civil Rights Act of 1964 and the Voting Rights Act of 1965; and it had little interest in Americans at the lower end of the income scale, especially blacks.

To African Americans, the most dramatic symbol of this was President Reagan's begrudging support of the effort to get the United States Congress to approve a national holiday in honor of Martin Luther King, Jr. When President Reagan left the White House in 1988, he was succeeded by George Bush, his former vice president. To most African

Americans, the four years of the Bush administration represented little or no change from the racial policies of the Reagan administration.

For many African Americans, the most positive political development of the Reagan-Bush years were the two dramatic and highly publicized, though unsuccessful, campaigns of the African-American leader Jesse Jackson for the Democratic presidential nomination. Few other events seemed to focus the attention of the black community on the value of the political process as a means of bringing their issues and concerns to the attention of the American people. Jackson's action and rhetoric generated hope in an African-American community reeling under the impact of severe unemployment, high levels of illegitimate births to young black women, rising rates of crime and violence, a drug epidemic, inadequate and increasingly ineffective public schools, an AIDS crisis, and numerous expressions of black popular culture that reflected a profound sense of alienation.

In the presidential campaign of 1992, with Jesse Jackson no longer a participant, African-American voters seemed to see in Bill Clinton, the Democratic presidential candidate, and his running mate, Al Gore, an interest in their problems that had not been evident during the Reagan and Bush years. Eighty-three percent of the African Americans who voted in November 1992 supported the victorious Clinton-Gore ticket.

REVIEW QUESTIONS

Chapter Content Review

1.   How did Ronald Reagan view both the Civil Rights Act of 1946 and the Voting Rights Act of 1965?

2.   Who was the first African American ever to become a full general in the United States military?

3. What African-American leader met with the president of Syria and the head of the Palestine Liberation Organization (PLO) in 1979? For what purpose?

4. Who was the winning presidential candidate in 1980? What percentage of the African-American vote did he receive?

5. Why did President Reagan withdraw the nomination of William Bell to chair the Equal Employment Opportunity Commission (EEOC)?

6. What were the actions that Jesse Jackson and his organization took to persuade the Coca-Cola Company and other businesses to increase the number of their black employees and expand services to the African-American community?

7. What was the public response to the Reagan administration's reversal in 1982 of an eleven-year policy in regard to the tax-exempt status of private educational and certain other nonprofit institutions?

8. What was the unemployment rate in the African-American community in 1982?

9. What was the cause and result of Jesse Jackson's trip to Syria in 1983?

10. What was the unemployment rate in the African-American community in 1985?

11. Who was the winning presidential candidate in 1988? For whom did the majority of African-Americans vote?

12. What was the decision of the U.S. Supreme Court in the case of *City of Richmond v. J. A. Crosson Company?*

13. Who was the first African American to be elected governor of Virginia? In what year was he elected?

14. Who was the first African American to be appointed chairman of the Joint Chiefs of Staff? In what year was he appointed? By whom was the appointment made?

15. What decisions did the U.S. Supreme Court render in *Patterson v. McLean Credit Union, Ward's Cove Packing Company v. Antonio,* and *Martin v. Wilks?* In what year or years were the cases decided? What was the importance of these cases to African-American history?

16. Why did President Bush veto the Civil Rights Bill passed by the United States Congress early in 1990? What caused him to sign, later in the same year, another version of the bill passed by the United States Congress?

17. Who was the African American nominated by President Bush to the U.S. Supreme Court? In what year did the nomination take place? What controversies arose in connection with this nomination? Was the nominee confirmed?

18. What is the "crossover phenomenon" and what are some examples of it?

Identification Questions

You should be able to describe the following key terms, concepts, individuals, and places and explain their significance:

1. Clarence Pendleton
2. Proposition 209
3. Louis Farrakhan
4. *The Bell Curve*
5. Douglas Wilder

6. Colin Powell
7. Louis W. Sullivan
8. *Patterson v. McLean Credit Union, Ward's Cove Company v. Antonio,* and *Martin v. Wilks*
9. Clarence Thomas
10. Anita Hill

Essay Questions

1. Discuss the race relations policies of the Reagan administration and the response of the African-American community to them.

2. Trace the history of Jesse Jackson's two campaigns for the presidential nomination of the Democratic Party. What impact did the two Jackson campaigns have on the African-American community and on the United States as a whole?

3. What were the most important ways in which President George Bush and his administration dealt with black Americans? In what ways did the African Americans communicate their views of President Bush and his racial policies?

SELF-TEST

Multiple-Choice

1. Which president of the United States, somewhat reluctantly, signed the bill establishing a national holiday in honor of Martin Luther King, Jr.?
   a. Richard Nixon
   b. Gerald Ford
   c. Jimmy Carter
   d. Ronald Reagan

2. Jesse Jackson was
   a. the leader of both Trans-Africa and the Department of Housing and Urban Development in the 1980s.
   b. the first African American to be appointed United States ambassador to the United Nations.
   c. opposed to the bill in Congress that created a national holiday in honor of Martin Luther King, Jr.
   d. a two-time campaigner for the Democratic Party's nomination for president of the United States.

3. The founder of the Black Entertainment Network was
   a. Muhammed Ali.
   b. Spike Lee.
   c. Berry Gordy.
   d. Robert Johnson.

4. All of the following were prominent black "crossover" artists in the 1980s or 1990s except
   a. Diana Ross.
   b. Michael Jackson.
   c. Ralph Ellison.
   d. Stevie Wonder.

5. The U.S. Supreme Court ruled in this decision that it was unconstitutional for a certain portion of public contracts to be set aside for minority contractors.
   a. *City of Richmond v. J.A. Crosson Company*
   b. *Wards Cove Packaging Company v. Antonio*
   c. *Martin v. Wilks*
   d. *Patterson v. McLean Credit Union*

6. Jesse Jackson's organization, PUSH, functioned primarily to
   a. criticize black Republicans.
   b. garner political support for liberal whites.
   c. press the business and financial community for economic parity for African Americans.
   d. promote black leadership in professional football.

7. The premier African-American playwright of the twentieth century was
   a. August Williams.
   b. Henry Gates.
   c. Hale Woodruff.
   d. Robert Johnson.

Fill-in-the-Blank

1. _____ was the director of such films as *She's Gotta Have It, Jungle Fever, and Malcom X.*

2. The Californian Proposition which forbade the use of race as a basis for admitting students to California colleges and universities was called _____.

3. African American soldier _____ served his country both as the National Security Adviser and as chairmen of the Joint Chiefs of Staff.

4. _____ is the controversial leader of the Nation of Islam.

True/False

1. Wynton Marsalis is known for his skill as a jazz and classical trumpet player.

2. The Congressional Black Caucus opposed the nomination of Clarence Thomas for Supreme Court Justice.

3. President Reagan believed that the states should be responsible for enforcing civil rights laws.

4. Toni Morrison is the author of several highly acclaimed novels, including *The Bluest Eye*.

Relevance Today

1. Jesse Jackson has been enormously successful in negotiating for the release of American captives with leaders of foreign nations hostile to the United States. Why would leaders from Syria, the Palestine Liberation Organization, and, most recently, Yugoslavia agree to meet with Jackson, an unrecognized representative of the United States? What motives could Jackson have for assuming this role?

2. African-American female writers since the 1960s have wielded increasing power and influence across the American landscape. What can account for the position of prominence these women have enjoyed? What implications does this have for blacks in general?

CHAPTER 25
HALF CENTURY OF CHANGE

THEMES AND MAJOR POINTS

For the African-American community, the closing decade of the twentieth century was a mixture of challenges and achievements.

An increase in the number of blacks holding elective and appointive offices on the national, state, and local levels steadily expanded the influence of African Americans in the political life of the United States. At the same time, debate over the place of blacks in the political process was as heated as it had been a generation earlier.

Changes in the population of the United States began to force African Americans to come to terms with the probability that by 2005 they would no longer be the largest minority group in the United States.

Many African Americans continued to feel a deep sense of connection with nonwhites in other parts of the world and used their political influence to urge the leaders of the United States to take a positive interest in people of color in foreign countries.

KEY EVENTS

1974   Rap music emerged as a distinctive expression of African American culture.

1977   Andrew Young, an African American was appointed United States Ambassador to the United Nations.

1981   AIDS began to have a major impact on the African-American community.

1984   On Thanksgiving day, four prominent African-American leaders
       began a sit-in in the South African Embassy to protest apartheid.

1985   Douglas Wilder was elected the first African-American lieutenant
       governor of Virginia.

1986   The National Black Gay and Lesbian Conference was established.

1988   Congress passed an Anti-Drug Abuse Act, leading to the
       appointment of the first "drug czar."

1989   Douglas Wilder was elected the first African-American governor
       of Virginia.
       George Bush appointed Colin Powell to the position of chairman
       of the Joint Chiefs of Staff.

1990   In June, Nelson Mandela, one of the most prominent leaders of the
       black South African liberation movement, made a twelve-day visit
       to the United States, during which he addressed a joint session of
       Congress.

1991   Congress authorized President Bush to use military force against
       Iraq and to expel it from Kuwait. Every African-American
       Democrat in Congress voted no.
       The first democratically elected president of Haiti was ousted:
       President Bush suspended aid to Haiti and refused to recognize the
       new regime.
       Earvin "Magic" Johnson and Arthur Ashe announced they were
       infected with the AIDS virus.
       In March, Rodney King, an African American, was arrested and
       beaten by police in Los Angeles; the beating was videotaped by a
       passerby.

1992   In March, the National Minority AIDS Council accused federal
       agencies of providing inadequate financial support to prevent the

spread of AIDS among Americans of African, Hispanic, Asian, and Native American ancestry.

The total number of African Americans in the U.S. House of Representatives reached thirty-nine.

President Clinton chose four African Americans to serve as cabinet officers.

1993   After the four policemen who arrested Rodney King were tried in federal court for violating King's civil rights, two were found guilty and two were acquitted.

Toni Morrison was awarded the Noble Prize for literary achievements.

CHAPTER OVERVIEW

For the African-American community, the closing decade of the twentieth century was a mixture of challenges and achievements. The considerable challenges included the impact on the black community of the widespread and growing use and abuse of drugs in all segments of American society, along with the attendant violence produced by proliferating drug markets and dealers in urban communities. As the century drew to a close, the AIDS crisis exacted a devastating toll of deaths among young blacks. Though this disease created a health crisis among other groups of Americans, the high rate of HIV infection and AIDS-related deaths among blacks made AIDS a major public health crisis in the African-American community. The AIDS crisis also forced a reluctant black community to begin to discuss the place of gays and lesbians within the African-American community. And the escalation in the number of incidents of police brutality against African Americans and barbarous assaults on minorities by criminal racists reinforced the arguments of blacks who declared that by century's end little or no progress had been made in race relations.

Other developments gave African Americans great pride and some hope for the future. In the last quarter of the century, the African-

American upper classes grew in both size and influence. The number of black millionaires and multimillionaires increased markedly and could be found in a wide variety of pursuits, including insurance, banking, manufacturing, publishing, retail, entertainment, sports, and communications. Many black high achievers also became celebrities and role models who received respect and, in some instances, even adulation from the American public. At the same time, there was a remarkable expansion in the number of blacks who held public office as elected and appointed officials.

The United States' relations with foreign countries were of great interest to black Americans, especially when they involved African nations or countries whose populations were of African descent. Whether the issue was the anti apartheid struggle in South Africa, the invasion of Panama, the threatened invasion of Haiti, the treatment of Haitian refugees seeking asylum in the United States, or the triumphal tour of President Bill Clinton and First Lady Hillary Rodham Clinton on the African continent, concerned African Americans followed events closely and made their opinions known to their elected representatives.

Chapter Content Review

1. What is rap music? What is its message?

2. By what year had AIDS been identified as a major public health issue for the African-American community?

3. What motivated four prominent African-American leaders to begin a sit-in at the South African Embassy in 1987?

4. When and for what purposes was the National Black Gay and Lesbian Conference established?

5. When and why did the United States Congress pass an Anti-Drug Abuse Act? What is a "drug czar"?

6. What message did Jesse Jackson send to the ruler of Panama in 1988? What was the response?

7. Who is Nelson Mandela? What was the purpose of his visit to the United States in 1990?

8. Who was the first democratically elected president of Haiti? What was President Bush's response to his ouster?

9. Who was the African American nominated by President Bush to the United States Supreme Court? In what year did the nomination take place? What controversies arose in connection with this nomination? Was the nominee confirmed?

10. Name the two African-American athletes who announced in 1991 that they were infected with the AIDS virus.

11. Who is Rodney King? When and why was he arrested and beaten by police in Los Angeles?

12. What was the cause or causes of the Los Angeles riot of 1992?

13. When and why did Earvin "Magic" Johnson resign from the National Commission on AIDS?

14. What percentage of the African-American vote did the Clinton-Gore ticket receive in the presidential election of 1992?

15. Who was the first African-American woman to be elected to the United States Senate? When was she elected? What state did she represent?

16. Who was the African American appointed chair of President-elect Bill Clinton's transition team?

17. What was the outcome of the federal trial of the four Los Angeles police officers accused on violating the civil rights of Rodney King?

18. How significant is the AIDS epidemic with respect to African Americans?

19. What challenges does the immigration of nonblack minorities pose for African Americans?

20. What was the primary focus of the advisory board on race relations appointed by Bill Clinton in 1997?

Identification Questions

You should be able to describe the following key terms, concepts, individuals, and places and explain their significance:

1. rap music
2. Daniel "Chappie" James
3. Andrew Young
4. William Bell
5. HIV
6. AIDS
7. *City of Richmond v. J. A. Crosson Company*
8. William Bennett
9. Harold Washington
10. Robert Goodman
11. apartheid
12. *Patterson v. McLean Credit Union, Ward Cove Company v. Antonio,* and *Martin v. Wilks*
13. "race-specific" scholarships
14. Rodney King
15. National Minority AIDS Council
16. Carol Moseley-Braun

17. Vernon Jordan
18. Dr. Jocelyn Elders
19. Michael Jordan
20. Sammy Sosa
21. Tiger Woods
22. Ronald Brown

Essay Questions

1. What were the three most difficult social problems faced by the African-American community at the turn of the twentieth century?

2. What do you think were the greatest strengths of the African-American community as it entered the new millennium?

3. Why did the new congressional districts created by congressional mandate that took race into consideration create such a controversy? Was this controversy resolved in a way that was fair to all involved?

4. What needed to be done in the United States to ensure that when African Americans ceased to be the largest minority in the United Sates this did not have a negative effect on any American ethnic or racial group?

5. Was "One America," the goal of President Bill Clinton and his advisory board on race, a realistic goal in the late twentieth or early twenty-first centuries?

6. Why did late-twentieth-century African Americans feel a deep sense of connection with nonwhites in other parts of the world? Was this good or bad for our nation?

SELF-TEST

Multiple-Choice

1. Each of the following was a problem plaguing African-American communities between 1980 and 2000 except
    a. HIV infection and AIDS.
    b. chronic unemployment.
    c. a lack of schools.
    d. a high level of illegitimate births among young women.

2. Which of the following men shattered Roger Maris's record for home runs in a season by hitting 66 and won the National League MVP Award?
    a. Sammy Sosa
    b. Tiger Woods
    c. Vernon Jordan
    d. Ronald Brown

3. This man, appointed United States Ambassador to the United Nations, demonstrated his commitment to racial justice by advocating majority rule in Rhodesia, South Africa, and other areas around the globe.
    a. Julian Bond
    b. Andrew Young
    c. Vernon Jordan
    d. Ronald Brown

4. The first African American ever to become a four-star general in the United States military was
    a. Daniel "Chappie" James.
    b. Colin Powell.
    c. Douglas Wilder.
    d. Rodney King.

5. In 1984, Randall Robinson and three other prominent African-American leaders began a sit-in at the embassy of South Africa to protest that nation's policy of apartheid. Who was the South African leader released from prison six years after this protest?
   a. Manuel Noriega
   b. Nelson Mandela
   c. Harold Washington
   d. Jesse Jackson

Fill-in-the-Blank

1. _____ is one of the two prominent African Americans who disclosed in 1991 that they were infected with AIDS.

2. _____ was the first female African American elected to the Senate of the United States.

3. _____ was the first democratically elected president of Haiti.

4. _____, a philosophy popular among many blacks, includes notions of African cultural superiority, creativity, and greatness.

5. The musical form, _____, popularized in the late 1980s and 1990s, expresses much of the rage, frustration, poverty, and violence common to urban blacks.

True/False

1. President Bush's response to the AIDS crisis in the 1980s was swift and decisive.

2. The members of President Clinton's advisory board on race relations agreed that the most pressing problem for African Americans involved winning more political offices.

3.   Maya Angelou was the first African-American woman ever elected to the United States Senate.

4.   President Bill Clinton named only one African American to serve in his cabinet.

5.   Rap music originated in the American South during the 1940s and 1950s.

Relevance Today

1.   There has been a marked trend in recent American history for significantly more African Americans than whites to voice opposition to U.S. military operations in foreign nations. How would you account for this discrepancy?

2.   With the recent trend of nonblack minority immigrants to move to urban centers in the United States, African Americans find themselves being in a unique position to offer advice and assistance. What lessons from the African-American past would you share with these recent immigrants and why? What accommodations have urban blacks successfully made to life in America since the 1960s, and could recent immigrants follow their strategies for success?

ANSWER KEY

Chapter 1

A.   Multiple-Choice
1.   a
2.   a
3.   b
4.   a
5.   c

B.   Fill-in-the-Blank
1.   2000
2.   Kanem and Bornu
3.   Europe and Asia
4.   various crafts and mining
5.   castle

C.   True/False
1.   false
2.   true
3.   true
4.   false
5.   true

Chapter 2

A.   Multiple-Choice
1.   a
2.   c
3.   a
4.   d
5.   b
6.   d

B.   Fill-in-the-Blank
1.   clan
2.   small kingdom
3.   Christians
4.   Arabic

C.   True/False
1.   true
2.   true
3.   true
4.   false
5.   false

Chapter 3

A.   Multiple-Choice
1.   a
2.   c
3.   c
4.   c
5.   a

B.   Fill-in-the-Blank
1.   Maroons
2.   Seasoning
3.   Indentured servants
4.   Estevanico
5.   the Viceroyalty of New Granada, comprising the modern states of Panama, Colombia, Venezuela, and Ecuador

C. True/False
1. false
2. true
3. true
4. false
5. true

Chapter 4

A. Multiple-Choice
1. d
2. c
3. b
4. b
5. c

B. Fill-in-the Blank
1. Virginia
2. Quakers, or Society of Friends
3. New England
4. South Carolina
5. Fundamental Constitution of the Carolinas
6. Carolinas or South Carolina

C. True/False
1. true
2. true
3. false
4. true

Chapter 5

A. Multiple-Choice
1. c
2. a
3. d
4. c
5. b

B. Fill-in-the-Blank
1. Georgia or South Carolina
2. Lord Dunmore
3. French and Indian
4. John Woolman
5. Rufus King

C. True/False
1. false
2. true
3. true
4. true
5. false

Chapter 6

A. Multiple-Choice
1. b
2. d
3. b
4. b
5. a
6. c

B. Fill-in-the-Blank
1. Vermont or Massachusetts
2. Eli Witney
3. Toussaint L'Ouverture
4. Richard Allen
5. Louisiana

C. True/False
1. true
2. false
3. false
4. false

Chapter 7

A. Multiple-Choice
1. b
2. c
3. c
4. b
5. a

B. Fill-in-the-Blank
1. James P. Beckwourth
2. Warhawks
3. Northwest Ordinance
4. Manifest Destiny
5. Woolfolk, Saunders, and Overly of Maryland and Franklin and Armfield of Virginia

C. True/False
1. false
2. true
3. false
4. true
5. false

Chapter 8

A. Multiple-Choice
1. b
2. d
3. a
4. d
5. d

B. Fill-in-the-Blank
1. planters
2. patrol
3. gang
4. Baptists or Methodists

C. True/False
1. false
2. false
3. true
4. true
5. false
6. false

Chapter 9

A.   Multiple-Choice
1. b
2. d
3. a
4. a
5. c

B.   Fill-in-the-Blank
1. Free
2. North Star
3. American Colonization Society
4. John C. Stanly
5. Fanny Kemble and Frederick L. Olmsted

C.   True/False
1. true
2. false
3. false
4. false
5. true

Chapter 10

A.   Multiple-Choice
1. c
2. c
3. b
4. c
5. d

B.   Fill-in-the-Blank
1. gag rule
2. Underground Railroad
3. colonization
4. Frederick Douglass
5. Samuel Cornish

C.   True/False
1. false
2. true
3. false
4. false
5. false

Chapter 11

A.   Multiple-Choice
1. c
2. d
3. c
4. d
5. d

B.   Fill-in-the-Blank
1. Maryland
2. Confiscation Act
3. General David Hunter
4. The Fifty-Fourth Massachusetts Regiment
5. President Abraham Lincoln

C. True/False
1. true
2. true
3. false
4. true
5. false

Chapter 12

A. Multiple-Choice
1. a
2. c
3. d
4. a
5. c

B. Fill-in-the-Blank
1. Thirteenth
2. black codes
3. Freedmen's Bureau
4. Homestead Act
5. Freedmen's Bank

C. True/False
1. false
2. true
3. true
4. true
5. true

Chapter 13

A. Multiple-Choice
1. d
2. d
3. b
4. c
5. a

B. Fill-in-the-Blank
1. Populists
2. Union League of America
3. Two of the following three: Florida, Louisiana, South Carolina
4. Tom Watson
5. Isaiah T. Montgomery

C. True/False
1. true
2. true
3. true
4. false
5. false

Chapter 14

A. Multiple-Choice
1. d
2. d
3. c
4. d
5. d

B. Fill-in-the-Blank
1. Booker T. Washington
2. Knights of Labor
3. W.E.B. Du Bois
4. Elijah McCoy
5. American Negro Academy

C. True/False
1. true
2. false
3. false
4. false
5. false

Chapter 15

A. Multiple-Choice
1. b
2. b
3. d
4. a
5. c

B. Fill-in-the-Blank
1. Charles Young
2. W.E.B. Du Bois
3. Urban League
4. Liberia
5. Minnie Cox

C. True/False
1. true
2. true
3. false
4. false
5. true

Chapter 16

A. Multiple-Choice
1. c
2. c
3. b
4. d
5. d

B. Fill-in-the-Blank
1. the 369th
2. *Messenger*
3. Emmett J. Scott
4. "The Battle of Henry Johnson"
5. France

C. True/False
1. false
2. false
3. true
4. true
5. false

Chapter 17

A. Multiple-Choice
1. b
2. a
3. d
4. a
5. d

B. Fill-in-the-Blank
1. "Red Summer"
2. Universal Negro Improvement Association (UNIA)
3. Brotherhood of Sleeping Car Porters and Maids
4. Ku Klux Klan
5. Rosewood

C. True/False
1. false
2. false
3. true
4. false
5. false

Chapter 18

A. Multiple-Choice
1. d
2. c
3. d
4. c
5. d
6. b

B. Fill-in-the-Blank
1. *Opportunity*
2. *Shuffle Along*
3. *The Green Pastures*
4. Aaron Douglas
5. Jessie Redmond Fauset

C. True/False
1. false
2. true
3. true
4. true

Chapter 19

A. Multiple-Choice
1. c
2. d
3. b
4. b
5. c

B. Fill-in-the-Blank
1. Scottsboro boys
2. John L. Lewis
3. A. Philip Randolph
4. the Tuskegee Study
5. Harlem/New York City

C. True/False
1. false
2. true
3. true
4. true
5. false

Chapter 20

A. Multiple-Choice
1. c
2. d
3. b
4. d
5. d
6. a

B. Fill-in-the-Blank
1. G. Carter Woodson
2. Earl Warren
3. Julius Rosenwald Fund
4. Richard Wright

C. True/False
1. false
2. true
3. false
4. false
5. false

Chapter 21

A. Multiple-Choice
1. a
2. c
3. d
4. d
5. b

B. Fill-in-the-Blank
1. A. Philip Randolph
2. 8802
3. B. O. Davis
4. The United Nations
5. Women Accepted for Voluntary Emergency Service, or WAVES

C. True/False
1. false
2. false
3. false
4. false
5. false

Chapter 22

A. Multiple-Choice
1. b
2. d
3. c
4. d
5. a

B. Fill-in-the-blank
1. "To Secure These Rights"
2. A. Philip Randolph; Willard Townsend
3. J. Waties Waring
4. Southern Manifesto
5. *Ebony*

C. True/False
1. false
2. true
3. true
4. true
5. false

Chapter 23

A. Multiple-Choice
1. d
2. c
3. d
4. c
5. d

B. Fill-in-the-Blank
1. Twenty-Fourth Amendment
2. Thurgood Marshall
3. de Facto
4. Allan Bakke
5. Shirley Chisholm

C. True/False
1. false
2. true
3. false
4. true
5. true

Chapter 24

A. Multiple-Choice
1. d
2. d
3. d
4. c
5. a
6. c
7. a

B. Fill-in-the-Blank
1. Spike Lee
2. 209
3. Colin Powell
4. Louis Farrakhan

C. True/False
1. true
2. true
3. true
4. true

Chapter 25

A. Multiple-Choice
1. c
2. a
3. b
4. b
5. b

B. Fill-in-the-Blank
1. Arthur Ashe; Earvin "Magic" Johnson
2. Carol Moseley-Braun
3. Jean-Bertrand Aristide
4. Afrocentricism
5. rap

C. True/False
1. false
2. false
3. false
4. false
5. false

NOTES

NOTES

NOTES

NOTES

NOTES

NOTES

NOTES

NOTES

NOTES